Christmas!

Appetizers Salads & Main Dishes

Bread Snowman

Wilton Snowman Pan
2 loaves (16 oz. each) frozen bread dough, thawed
1/2 teaspoon garlic powder
1 teaspoon dill weed

To thaw bread dough, place in plastic bag at room temperature for 4-6 hours. Or let thaw overnight in refrigerator. Grease Snowman Pan with solid vegetable shortening. Combine loaves and knead together with seasonings. Form into oblong loaf. Press in greased pan and let raise until doubled in size.

Bake at 350° for 25-35 minutes or until golden brown.

Remove bread from pan and cool. Trim top so that snowman rests flat on tray. Hollow out belly and reserve trimmed bread for dipping. Cut reserved bread in cubes, spoon dip into snow-man. Serve with carrot sticks, celery, zucchini and bread cubes.

To decorate snowman: for tie, dip green top of leek into boiling water or place in microwave 30 seconds to soften. Place on Snowman. Use black olives for eyes, small carrot for nose, parsley for hat trim.

Spinach Dip

1 1/4 cup sour cream
3/4 cup mayonnaise
1/2 teaspoon black pepper
1/2 teaspoon salt
1 teaspoon dried basil
1/2 teaspoon chopped fresh or dried dill
1/4 teaspoon garlic powder
1/4 cup chopped green onion
1/4 cup shredded carrots
1 (16 oz.) package chopped spinach, thawed and drained
3/4 cup chopped roasted walnuts

Combine ingredients in order listed. Dip can be made a day before serving; cover and refrigerate. If made ahead, add nuts just before serving.

To roast nuts, spread on cookie sheet and place in a 350° oven for 8-10 minutes.

Try the bread idea above with the Snowman or another great Wilton wintertime pan. The Treeliteful or Star Pan will make an ideal party presentation. And don't forget, the bread can always be baked ahead and frozen until you need it.

Potato Caviar Wreaths

Wilton Tips 14, 15
2 lbs. small red potatoes
1 cup sour cream
Red and black caviar
Fresh dill and parsley

Scrub potatoes and boil with skins on approximately 15-20 minutes. Do not overcook; skins should not be split. Cool and slice into 1/4 in. thick slices. Pipe sour cream wreaths, zigzags and stars with tip 14 and 15 star tip. Garnish with caviar, dill and parsley. Makes 50-60.

Festive Croutons

Wilton Nesting Star and Round Cookie Cutter Sets
1 loaf unsliced firm bread
Olive oil or olive oil cooking spray
Herbs: parsley, dill and/or basil

Remove crusts from bread; slice in 1/4 or 1/3 inch thick slices. Cut with star cutters. Brush or spray cookie sheet with olive oil and place bread stars in one layer. Spray or brush tops with olive oil. Sprinkle with herbs, if desired. Serve with holiday cheese trays, as salad croutons or as bases for piped cheeses, meats or vegetable spreads. Makes 100-120.

Tomato Bruschetta

Looking for a deliciously different party spread? This easy-to-fix mixture (not shown) can be made ahead and stored tightly covered in the refrigerator.

1 pound ripe plum tomatoes, seeded and chopped, or
1-26 oz. can peeled and chopped plum tomatoes, well drained
1/2 fennel bulb, cleaned and chopped
1/3 cup coarsely chopped fresh basil
1 garlic clove, finely chopped
1/2 teaspoon salt
1/4 teaspoon black pepper
Croutons rubbed with a peeled garlic clove while warm

Mix all ingredients except croutons. Use as spread with croutons. Serve warm.

You can create small bread wreaths by using two sizes of our nesting round cutters. On a 1/4 in. thick slice of bread, first cut the larger circle, then the smaller inner edges. Pipe on a cream cheese topping and decorate with green olives, pimentos, red pepper or parsley.

Apricot Baked Brie

Wilton 4-pc. Nesting Christmas Tree Set
1 egg
1 tablespoon water
1 whole chilled baby brie
1/4 cup apricot preserves
1 sheet frozen puff pastry

Preheat oven to 375^0. Mix egg with water. Thaw puff pastry; unfold and roll on lightly floured surface to approximately 14 in. square. Brush brie with apricot preserves. Place on rolled pastry. Trim pastry to circle. Cut leaves from extra pastry with small tree cutter from Wilton 4-pc. Nesting Christmas Tree Set. Reserve. Brush pastry edges around brie with egg. Fold remaining pastry over brie and trim as necessary. Place on baking sheet seam side down. Brush top with egg and place leaves around top. Brush again with egg mixture, bake 25 minutes or until pastry is puffed and golden. Cool for 15-20 minutes before serving.

Cheese Trees

Wilton Spritz Cookie Press
1 lb. (natural, not processed) sharp cheddar or aged swiss, finely shredded
1/2 cup butter, softened
2 teaspoons Worcestershire sauce
dash of hot red pepper sauce
1 1/2 cups flour
1/2 teaspoon salt
1 teaspoon paprika

Preheat oven to 375^0. In a medium mixer bowl, cream the cheese†, butter, Worcestershire sauce and hot red pepper sauce until smooth. In separate bowl, toss flour and seasonings with fork. Gradually add to cheese mixture. Mix until dough holds together and shape into small logs.

Place in Wilton Spritz Cookie Press and press trees onto ungreased cookie sheet. Bake 10-12 minutes or until lightly browned. Remove and cool on rack. Makes 4 dozen.

†Do not use pre-shredded packaged cheese.

Use the Wilton Spritz Cookie Press when you're pressed for time during the holidays. The cheese trees above are a great make-ahead idea. They can be stored at room temperature up to 1 week in an airtight container, or frozen for up to 2 months. You'll find 9 other great holiday shapes included with the press!

Molded Waldorf Salad

For a new twist on the traditional Waldorf salad, mold it!

Wilton Viennese Swirl Pan
3 (3 oz.) pkgs. cherry gelatin
3 cups boiling water
2 1/4 cups cold water
1 1/2 cups chopped celery
1 1/2 cups coarsely chopped walnuts, toasted
2 1/2 cups chopped apple, unpeeled
1 (3 oz.) pkg. lemon gelatin
1 cup boiling water
3/4 cup cold water
1/4 cup mayonnaise
1/4 cup sour cream

Lightly oil Viennese Swirl Pan. In a large bowl add boiling water to cherry gelatin; stir until dissolved. Add cold water. Chill until slightly thickened; fold in celery, walnuts and apples. Pour into prepared pan. Chill until top is firm (2-3 hours).

In a mixing bowl add boiling water to lemon gelatin; stir until dissolved. Add cold water. Blend in mayonnaise and sour cream with wire whip. Pour on top of firm cherry/apple layer. Chill until firm, at least four hours or overnight.

To serve, dip pan in warm water to rim for 2-3 seconds. Unmold on serving plate. Repositioning mold will be easy if you dampen the serving plate with cold water before unmolding gelatin. Serve with additional mayonnaise flavored with grated lemon rind. Makes 16 servings.

Our Viennese Swirl Pan bakes Christmas desserts plain or fancy. A simple pound cake takes elegant shape un-iced and topped with fruit. And the Choco-Great Cake with chocolate glaze is a rich finish, trimmed with whipped cream and raspberries. The recipe is on the label.

Salmon Mousse

Wilton Treeliteful Pan
2 lbs. fresh salmon
2 cups water
2 tablespoons unflavored gelatin (3 packets)
1 cup reserved salmon broth
1 teaspoon nutmeg
1 teaspoon salt
1/4 teaspoon pepper
1 teaspoon Worcestershire sauce
1 tablespoon chopped fresh dill or 1 teaspoon dried
1/2 cup mayonnaise
1/2 cup sour cream
1/2 cup dry white wine
1 cup whipping cream, whipped
1/8 teaspoon liquid smoke sauce (optional)

Place salmon in pan with water, bring to boil, cover and simmer 15 minutes or until fish flakes easily with fork. Remove salmon from broth and cool. Reserve one cup broth. When salmon is cool, remove skin and bones; break fish into small pieces.

Soften gelatin in reserved broth, heat until dissolved. Place fish into food processor bowl fitted with metal blade. Process while gradually adding gelatin mixture. Add seasonings (including liquid smoke sauce, if desired) and process until mixture is of a paste consistency.

Transfer mixture to large mixing bowl. Stir in mayonnaise, sour cream and wine. Refrigerate until mixture has partially set. Fold in whipped cream. Pour into lightly oiled Treeliteful Pan; level. Cover and refrigerate until firm, at least 8 hours.

To remove from pan, carefully loosen edges with a small spatula and invert onto serving plate. Garnish with star croutons (pg. 7), parsley, cucumber bells and leek bows. Serve with cucumber sauce.

Makes 10-12 buffet servings or 25 appetizer size servings.

NOTE: Fresh salmon can be white to pale pink or salmon color. If you would like a pinker color add a small amount of Wilton Red Color.

Cucumber Sauce

1 large cucumber, peeled and seeded
1/2 cup mayonnaise
1 cup sour cream
4 tablespoons chopped fresh dill or 2 teaspoons dried
2 tablespoons lemon juice
1/2 teaspoon ground black pepper
1/2 teaspoon salt
1 teaspoon Dijon mustard

Grate cucumber, drain and mix with remaining ingredients.

Cover and chill at least 4 hours before serving.

The Treeliteful Pan is an all-time Wilton bestseller! This durable aluminum pan makes much more than just cakes. Try a Holiday Hero, using your favorite hot roll mix, cold cuts and cheeses. Follow directions for baking on Bread Snowman (page 4). When cool, split bread and add fillings.

STAR BRUNCH CHEESE PUFF

Serve this easy dish immediately after baking.
Although it will lose air as it sets, it will taste wonderful!

For Filling:
10 oz. mild or hot fresh Italian sausage, casing removed, in 1/2 in. pieces
1/2 large onion, chopped
4 oz. fresh mushrooms, sliced
2 large tomatoes, coarsely chopped, or 1 (16 oz.) can whole tomatoes, drained and coarsely chopped
1 teaspoon dried basil
1/2 teaspoon salt

Saute sausage in 10 in. skillet; drain all but one tablespoon fat. Add onions and mushrooms, saute lightly. Add remainder of filling ingredients and simmer 10 minutes. Set aside while making shell. Filling may be made a day ahead, covered and refrigerated. Reheat before adding to shell.

For Puff Shell:
Wilton Star Pan
1 cup milk
1/2 cup butter
1 cup all-purpose flour
5 large eggs
2/3 cup diced cheddar cheese

Preheat oven to 375°. Grease the Star Pan with vegetable shortening. Bring milk and butter to boil in large saucepan. Remove from heat; add flour all at once and beat vigorously a few minutes until mixture is smooth and pulls away from sides of pan.

Cool mixture 3 or 4 minutes; beat in eggs one at a time. (This step may be done with a mixer.) After eggs have been beaten in, add cheese and mix. Cheese may still be in small chunks. Spread dough in pan, leaving a center well for filling. Spoon in warm filling. Bake at 375° for 25 minutes, or until puffed and brown. Makes 6 servings.

The puff, or gougère, has a souffle-like texture which requires a quality pan to properly rise. The Star Pan is all quality aluminum, to bake one cake mix or savory party entrees with perfect results.

Fettucine Wreath

Wilton 10 in. Ring Mold Pan
2 (12 oz.) packages dried spinach fettucine

Oil 10 in. Ring Mold Pan. Cook fettucine according to package directions. Drain, do not rinse, and pack into mold by pressing firmly on noodles with back of spoon. Unmold onto serving platter; add sauce and meatballs. After unmolding, fettucine can be kept warm by covering with foil and placing in a 250° oven for up to 30 minutes. Makes 8 servings.

Meatballs

2 lbs. ground sirloin
10 oz. hot Italian sausage, casings removed
2 teaspoons dried parsley
2 teaspoons dried basil
1/2 teaspoon garlic powder
1/2 teaspoon black pepper
1/2 cup finely chopped onion
2 eggs

Break ground beef apart with fork, add sausage. Add remaining ingredients and mix gently but thoroughly. Shape into one inch balls. Saute in large skillet one layer at a time until brown. Add to sauce.

Italian Pasta Sauce

1/4 cup olive oil
1 cup chopped onion
3 garlic cloves, chopped
1 tablespoon chopped fresh basil or 1 teaspoon dried
3 bay leaves
1/2 teaspoon black pepper
1/2 cup beef broth
1 teaspoon salt
2 (6 oz.) cans tomato paste
3 (15 oz.) cans whole Italian tomatoes, undrained
1 tablespoon sugar

Heat oil in large heavy saucepan. Saute onion and garlic until soft, but not brown. Add remaining ingredients and simmer 1 1/2 -2 hours, add meatballs and reheat.

Sauce and meatballs may be made a day ahead, refrigerated and reheated before adding to Fettucine Wreath.

The Wilton Ring Mold Pan also makes rice look more festive for your holiday buffet. Simply pack with cooked rice and unmold as above, for serving with creamed seafood or chicken dishes.

Zucchini/Pepper Pizza with Whole Wheat Crust

For Whole Wheat Pizza Dough:

Pizza Primo 16 1/2 in. Pizza Pan
1 Pkg. active dry yeast
1/2 cup warm water (110°)
1 cup all-purpose flour
1 cup whole wheat flour
1 teaspoon salt
2/3 cup milk

Dissolve yeast in water; set aside. In large mixing bowl, combine flours and salt.

Make a well in center of flour. Add yeast mixture and milk; mix together until dough forms ball. Turn out onto floured surface. Knead 4-6 minutes until dough is smooth. Shape dough into ball and place in oiled bowl, turning dough to coat. Cover, let rise in warm place for 1 1/2 hours, until doubled in bulk. Punch dough down, knead for 2 minutes. Roll out dough in 15 in.-17 in. diam. circle.

For pizza sauce:

1 tablespoon olive oil
2 cloves garlic, chopped
28 oz. can Italian plum tomatoes, drained, coarsely crushed
1 teaspoon oregano
1 teaspoon basil
1/2 teaspoon salt
1/2 teaspoon pepper

Saute chopped garlic in olive oil until softened, not browned. Add tomatoes, seasonings. Cook about 10 minutes until liquid evaporates.

For pizza topping:

12 oz. (3 cups) shredded mozzarella or fontina cheese
3 tablespoons olive oil
2 medium zucchini, sliced
1 medium onion, sliced
1/2 green and 1/2 red pepper, cut in strips
1 teaspoon dried or
1 tablespoon fresh basil

Lightly saute zucchini, peppers and onions in 1 tablespoon olive oil.

Preheat oven to 450°. Lightly brush pizza pan with olive oil. Place rolled out dough in pan; fold edge of dough to form raised edge. Lightly brush dough with olive oil. Bake 5 minutes; remove from oven and add sauce, cheese and toppings. Bake on bottom rack for 20-25 minutes or until edge is brown and cheese is bubbly.

Pizza is an easy holiday appetizer-the sauce and toppings pick up all the Christmas colors! Wilton pizza products make pizza tastier and more festive. Our pizza pan has an exclusive raised design to bake up a crispier crust.

Merry Christmas

Breads & Muffins

Christmas Fruit Bread

A perfect bread served warm with butter for Breakfast or Brunch.
Cooled and sliced, it also makes wonderful toast.

Wilton 6 in. Springform Pans
5 cups all-purpose flour
2 packages fast-rising yeast
1/3 cup sugar
Grated peel of 1 lemon
1 1/2 teaspoons salt
1 cup water
3/4 cup butter
5 egg yolks, lightly beaten
1 cup white raisins
3/4 cup dried tart cherries or diced dried apricots
2 tablespoons butter, melted

Grease two 6 in. Springform pans. Reserve one cup flour. Mix flour, yeast, sugar, grated peel and salt in large mixer bowl. Heat water and butter until hot to touch (125-130°F). Stir hot liquid into flour mixture. Mix in egg yolks. Add only enough reserved flour to make soft dough. On floured surface, knead 5 minutes or until dough is smooth and no longer sticky. Cover dough and let rest 10 minutes. Knead in raisins and cherries. Divide dough in half. Shape into flat balls, place in Springform pans and let rise until double in size.

Preheat oven to 400°. Brush top of loaves with melted butter and bake 10 minutes, reduce heat to 350° and bake an additional 40-45 minutes, or until browned. Cool 5 minutes, remove Springform, brush again with butter and serve warm, or cool.

Wilton Springform pans have a waffled bottom for strong support of thick holiday cheesecakes. And check the label for a colorful Christmas treat—a cherry-topped New York style cheesecake!

Onion Cheese Bread

Wilton Mini-Loaf Pan
3 tablespoons butter or margarine
1/2 cup chopped onion
3 cups all-purpose flour
1 tablespoon baking powder
1 teaspoon salt
1/4 teaspoon pepper
1 1/2 cups milk
2 cups (8 oz.) shredded cheddar cheese
3 tablespoons chopped green chilies

Preheat oven to 350°. Grease Mini-Loaf Pan, or spray with vegetable oil spray. Saute onion in butter until limp and transparent, not brown; set aside. Combine flour, baking powder, salt and pepper in large mixing bowl. Add remaining ingredients, including butter mixture, stir until just moistened; do not over mix. Divide batter in 6 cavity Mini-Loaf Pan. Bake 30-35 minutes or until browned and toothpick inserted in center comes out clean. Cool 5 minutes, remove from pan.

YIELD: 6 Mini-Loaves.

Lemon-Carrot Tea Bread

Wilton Mini-Loaf Pan
3/4 cup butter, softened
1 1/2 cups sugar
3 eggs
2 1/4 cups all-purpose flour
1/4 teaspoon salt
1/2 teaspoon soda
2 teaspoons baking powder
1/2 cup milk
1 tablespoon lemon juice
2 tablespoons grated lemon rind
3/4 cup chopped pecans
1 cup grated carrots

Preheat oven to 350°. Grease and flour Mini-Loaf Pan. Cream butter and sugar in large mixer bowl until light and fluffy. Add eggs and beat. Combine flour, salt, soda and baking powder, toss with fork to combine. Combine milk and lemon juice. Add alternately with flour to creamed mixture. Start and end with milk. Mix only until ingredients are moistened. Mix in lemon rind, pecans and carrots. Fill pans approximately 2/3 full. Bake 30-40 minutes, cool 5 minutes, remove from pans. Cool completely and wrap. May be frozen for 2 months.

YIELD: 8 loaves.

The Mini-Loaf Pan makes it easy to be Santa for everyone at your holiday table. Make your favorite fruitcake recipe, wrap each loaf in colored cellophane, label with each guest's name. Place on each plate for a festive place setting.

Cinnamon Bear

Wilton Panda Pan
Wilton 8 in. Square Pan
8 cups all-purpose flour
2 packages fast-rising yeast
1/2 cup sugar
3/4 teaspoon salt
1 1/2 cups water
1 1/2 cups butter
3 eggs, lightly beaten
2 tablespoons butter, melted
1/2 cup sugar
1 tablespoon ground cinnamon

Reserve 1 cup flour. Mix remaining flour, yeast, sugar and salt in large mixing bowl. Heat water and butter until hot to touch (125-130°F). Stir hot liquid into flour mixture, mix in beaten eggs. Add reserved flour to make a soft dough. On floured surface, knead 10-15 minutes until smooth and elastic. Cover dough and let rest 10 minutes. Roll out dough on floured surface to 15 x 18 in. rectangle. Brush surface with melted butter, sprinkle sugar and cinnamon evenly over surface. Roll from long edge, pinch ends together to seal. Shape into 16 in. long loaf. Divide in half. Cut half of dough into 1 in. slices for cinnamon rolls. Place in greased 8 in. square pan, cover. Let rise 45 minutes or until double in size. Cut 1 in. slice from remaining half, cut slice in half. Grease front and back of Panda Pan. Do not use core. Place dough in back half of pan, press dough to general shape of pan. Place one half of slice in each bottom paw; cut cinnamon surface should face upward. Cut an 18 x 12 in. piece of foil; fold into an approximately 5 in. square. Place foil inside opening in end of pan between dough and pan, foil should be large enough to go inside upper half of pan. When pan halves are clipped together, foil should completely cover opening in end of pan. Attach front half of pan with clips. Tuck foil inside top half. Let rise about 45 minutes in a warm place or until doubled in size. Dough will be about 1 in. from top of Panda Pan and will finish rising as it bakes.

Preheat oven to 350°. Bake rolls 20-25 minutes, Bear 40-45 minutes.

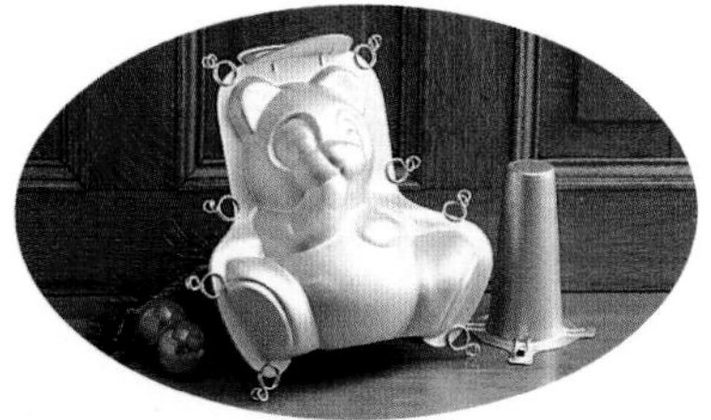

The Panda Pan lets you create a beautiful 3-D centerpiece for the holidays. Make cake according to directions on label, decorate with festive colors and set in the middle of your dessert or dinner table.

Bear Sandwiches

Wilton Mini Bear Pan
1 package (16 oz.) hot roll mix
1/4 cup mayonnaise
2 tablespoons mustard
2 tablespoons honey
12 (1 oz.) slices Swiss cheese
2 lbs. sliced ham
lettuce

Prepare hot roll mix according to package directions, up to shaping rolls. Divide dough into twelve equal pieces*. Grease Mini Bear Pan with solid vegetable shortening or use a vegetable pan spray. Form dough into flat oblongs and press into pan; the surface of dough toward bottom of pan should be very smooth. Cover and let rise in warm place until doubled in bulk, approximately 30 minutes. Bake at 375° for 15-20 minutes or until browned. Cool 5 minutes in pan and remove to rack to cool. In a small bowl mix mayonnaise, mustard and honey until smooth. When bread is cool split and spread with honey-mustard, top with ham, cheese and lettuce. Makes 12 sandwiches.

*If using one pan, refrigerate 6 pieces of dough until first six have baked. Then follow directions for rising and baking.

Hamburger Bears

1 package (16 oz) hot roll mix
2 tablespoons sesame seeds
3 lbs. ground beef

Follow above instructions for making dough. After greasing pan, sprinkle with sesame seeds, then place dough in pan. Follow remaining directions for rising, baking and cooling.

Form meat into twelve triangle shaped patties. Grill or broil and serve on split sesame buns. Makes 12 hamburgers.

The Mini Bear Pan never hibernates! You'll use it throughout the year for birthdays, baby showers and after school treats. One cake mix makes 12-16 little cubs.

Apple Tree Cake

Serve warm for Brunch or Dinner with
softly whipped cream and a dusting of cinnamon.

Wilton Treeliteful Pan
1 cup sugar
3 eggs
2 cups flour
1 1/2 teaspoons baking powder
3/4 cup butter or margarine, melted
1/2 cup milk
3/4 teaspoon vanilla extract
3 apples
1/4 cup sugar
1 1/2 teaspoons cinnamon

Preheat oven to 375°. Grease Treeliteful Pan with vegetable shortening or use vegetable pan spray. In a medium mixing bowl, beat sugar and eggs lightly. In a separate bowl, toss flour and baking powder with fork. To sugar and egg mixture, add 1/3 flour, melted butter, combine; then add another 1/3 flour; combine. Add milk, vanilla, remaining flour, mix until batter is smooth. Pour into prepared pan. Core and cut apples into eighths, or smaller for very large apples. Place apples on top of batter with rounded side up. Sprinkle with cinnamon sugar mixture. Bake 35-40 minutes or until toothpick inserted in center comes out clean. Cool 10 minutes on rack, remove from pan. 12 servings.

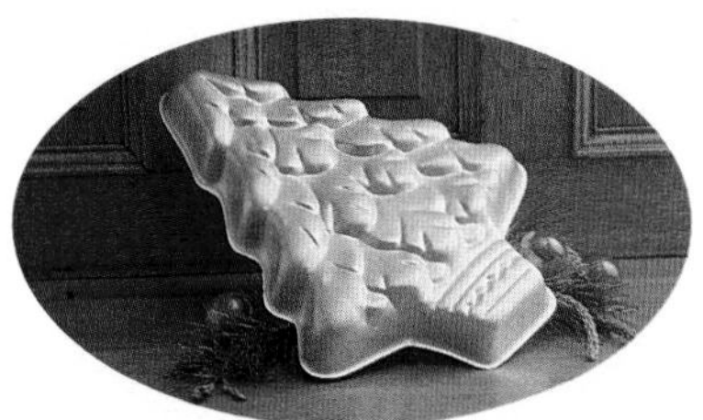

For a truly festive holiday punch, use the Treeliteful pan to create a floating "ice sculpture." Fill the pan with water (may be colored with a few drops of food coloring). Add cherries and assorted fruits. Freeze until solid. Unmold and float in your favorite punch.

Corn Muffins

Wilton Mini Tree Pan or Wilton Mini Muffin Pan
1 cup flour
1 cup cornmeal
3 tablespoons sugar
4 teaspoons baking powder
1 teaspoon salt
1 cup milk
$^1/_4$ cup oil
1 egg, slightly beaten
1 (11 oz.) can corn, well drained

Heat oven to 400^0. Spray pan with non-stick vegetable oil. In medium bowl combine first 5 ingredients. Stir in remaining ingredients, except corn, beat just until smooth. Fold in corn and pour batter into prepared pan. Bake 15 minutes; reduce temperature to 350^0 and bake additional 20 minutes. Makes 24 mini muffins.

Apple Cinnamon Muffins

Wilton Mini Tree Pan or Wilton Muffin Pans
2 $^1/_4$ cups flour
$^1/_2$ cup granulated sugar
3 teaspoons baking powder
1 teaspoon cinnamon, divided
$^1/_2$ teaspoon salt
2 eggs
$^3/_4$ cup milk
1 $^1/_2$ cups apple, peeled, finely chopped
$^1/_3$ cup melted butter
$^1/_3$ cup chopped pecans
$^1/_4$ cup firmly packed brown sugar

Combine flour, sugar, baking powder, $^1/_2$ teaspoon cinnamon and salt in large bowl. Beat eggs with milk. Stir in apple and butter. Add all at once to flour mixture; stir just until moist, batter will be very stiff. Spray pan with vegetable spray and fill $^2/_3$ full. Combine nuts, brown sugar and remaining $^1/_2$ teaspoon cinnamon. Sprinkle over each muffin. Bake in 350^0 oven for 30 minutes. Makes 9-12 trees; 12 standard muffins.

Everyone loves to top our Mini Trees! Make single serving cakes in the Mini Tree Pan and let the kids frost and decorate them to their hearts' desire. Pumpkin or cranberry breads work wonderfully in this pan too!

Cranberry Wheat-Nut Muffins

Wilton Muffin Pans, jumbo standard or mini sizes
1 cup whole wheat flour
1 cup all-purpose flour
1/2 tsp. salt
1 cup firmly packed brown sugar
1/2 cup butter
2 eggs
3/4 cup sour cream
1 tsp. baking soda
2 cups fresh cranberries, coarsely chopped
1/2 cup chopped walnuts

Preheat oven to 350°. Grease and flour muffin pans or line with paper baking cups. Combine flours and salt, toss with fork, set aside. Cream sugar and butter in large mixing bowl. Add eggs one at a time, beating well after each addition. Add soda to sour cream; stir. Add sour cream and flour mixture alternately to batter. Mix only until traces of flour disappear. Fold in cranberries and nuts. Fill prepared muffin pan 3/4 full.

Makes 6 Jumbo Muffins (Bake 30-40 minutes), 18 Standard Muffins (Bake 20-30 minutes), or 60 Mini Muffins (Bake 15-20 minutes).

Refrigerator Bran Muffins

This muffin is not pictured but is ideal to have in your refrigerator for quick but special Holiday Breakfasts. The batter can be kept up to 4 weeks tightly covered in the refrigerator.

Wilton Standard Muffin Pan
1 cup boiling water
2 cups bran flakes cereal
1 cup 100% bran cereal
1 1/4 cups sugar
1/2 cup vegetable shortening
2 eggs
2 cups buttermilk
3 cups flour
1/2 teaspoon salt
2 1/2 teaspoon baking soda
1 teaspoon vanilla

Pour boiling water over bran flakes cereal and set aside. Place sugar and shortening in large mixing bowl, cream until fluffy, add eggs and mix. Add buttermilk, mix. Stir together flour, salt and baking soda, add to sugar mixture and mix until smooth. Add vanilla, 100% bran and cereal which has been soaking in water. Stir until all ingredients are mixed in.

Bake in paper muffin cups or grease and flour pan or use vegetable pan spray.

Bake immediately or store batter in tightly covered glass or plastic container in the refrigerator for up to 4 weeks.

Add 1 cup chopped apples, nuts, or raisins when ready to bake. Bake at 400° for 25-35 minutes. Makes 1 dozen muffins.

Entertaining options are endless with the wide variety of Wilton muffin pans. Jumbo, regular and mini muffins will go from dinner parties to children's parties with ease. For an added festive touch, line muffin pans with Wilton holiday-patterned baking cups.

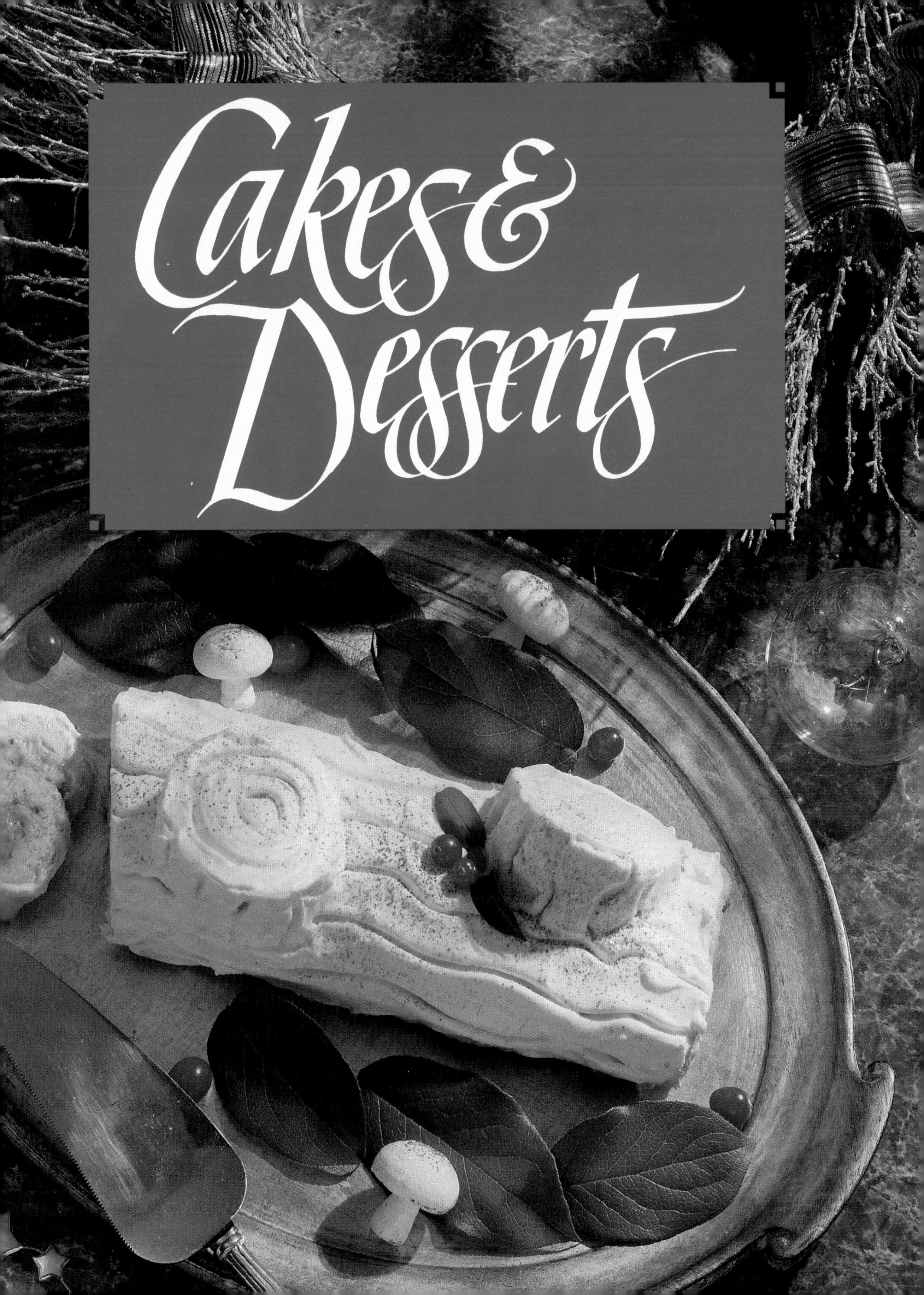
Cakes & Desserts

OH CHRISTMAS TREE!

Wilton 10 in. Round Pan
Wilton Tips 7, 11, 17, 352
Wilton Kelly Green Icing Color
Wilton Decorating Comb
Wilton Cake Dividing Set
Wilton Fanci-Foil Wrap, Cake Board
Wilton Tree Former Set
Candy-Coated Mini Chocolate Pieces
16 Small Candy Canes
Buttercream icing (see p. 42)
Royal icing (below)

FOR TREE: With royal icing cover waxed paper-covered tree former with tip 352 leaves, trim with candy-coated chocolate pieces. Let dry.

Ice 2-layer cake smooth, then comb sides with small ridged edge of decorating comb. Using cake dividing set, mark sides into 10ths, connect with tip 17 zigzag garland. Overpipe with tip 352 leaves and trim with candy-coated chocolate pieces. Edge top with tip 7 and bottom with tip 11 bead borders.

Position tree and candy canes on cake top. 24 servings.

ROYAL ICING

3 level tablespoons Wilton Meringue Powder
4 cups sifted confectioners sugar (approx. 1 lb.)
*6 tablespoons water**

Beat all ingredients at low speed for 7 to 10 minutes (10 to 12 minutes at high speed for portable mixer) until icing forms peaks.
Makes 3 cups.

*When using large counter top mixer or for stiffer icing, use 1 tablespoon less water.

NOTE: Royal icing pieces made ahead should be stored at room temperature out of direct light.

The Wilton 10 in. Round Pan is perfectly sized for one two-layer cake recipe or mix. For added holiday fun, make two or three layers (each a different flavor) and fill with Wilton Cake and Pastry Filling, whipped topping or icing.

Mr. Snowman

Wilton Snowman Pan
Wilton Tips 4, 15, 17, 233
Wilton Black, No-Taste Red, Kelly Green Icing Colors
Wilton Cake Board, Fanci-Foil Wrap

Outline hat, mouth, scarf, vest and holly leaves with tip 4. Pipe tip 4 dot eyes and nose. Cover hat band with two tip 17 stripes. Overpipe band with tip 4 strings to form squares. Cover hat, face, scarf, vest and body with tip 17 stars. Cover holly leaves with tip 15 stars, pipe tip 4 holly berries. Add tip 233 pull out "fur" for earmuffs and tip 4 dot buttons. 12 servings.

Meet The Mrs.

Wilton Snowman Pan
Wilton Tips 3, 4, 15, 17, 104
Wilton Black, Kelly Green, No-Taste Red Icing Colors
Wilton Cake Boards, Fanci-Foil Wrap

To create grey hair effect, use a spatula to stripe inside of decorating bag with black icing. Next, fill bag with white icing. Pipe side-by-side strings with tip 17 for hair and bun. Overpipe as necessary for dimension. Outline mouth, cape, arms, dress and holly leaves with tip 4. Pipe in dots for eyes, nose, cheeks, buttons, holly berries and lips with tip 4. Cover face, arms, dress, body with tip 17 stars. Fill in holly leaves with tip 15 stars, pipe tip 4 berries. Add tip 104 ruffle to cape and dress hem. Trim neckline and top of ruffles with tip 3 beads. Add tip 3 string bow at neckline. 12 servings.

For a quick and easy children's treat try the Snow Crunch Couple. Prepare marshmallow crisp rice cereal treat recipe according to directions on cereal box. Spray Snowman Pan with vegetable pan spray. Pack mixture into pan and let set. Have children help decorate features with festive candy.

Rosy Wreath

Wilton 11 x 15 in. Sheet Pan
Wilton Oval Pan Set (11 1/4 x 8 1/2 in. used as pattern)
Wilton Tips 5, 7, 12, 102, 125, 301, 352
Wilton Christmas Red, Kelly Green, Ivory Icing Colors
Flower Nail No. 7
Buttercream Icing (below), (make 3 recipes)
Royal Icing (p. 39)

Using royal icing and tips 7 and 102, make 16 large roses, 12 medium and 8 rosebuds. Let dry. Ice cake smooth. Lightly press oval pan to imprint wreath pattern; or make a free-hand oval, outlined with a toothpick. Write tip 301 message. With tip 12 build up oval outline for wreath on cake.
Pipe tip 352 leaves on wreath. Add tip 352 leaf border to bottom, tip 5 bead border to top. Use tip 125 to make wreath bow. Position roses and rosebuds and add tip 352 leaf accents.
22 servings.

Buttercream Icing

1/2 cup solid vegetable shortening
*1/2 cup butter or margarine**
1 tsp. Wilton Clear Vanilla Extract
4 cups sifted confectioners sugar (approx. 1 lb.)
*2 tablespoons milk***

Cream butter and shortening with electric mixer. Add vanilla. Gradually add sugar, one cup at a time, beating well on medium speed. Scrape sides and bottom of bowl often. When all sugar has been mixed in, icing will appear dry. Add milk and beat at medium speed until light and fluffy. Keep icing covered with a damp cloth until ready to use. For best results, keep icing bowl in refrigerator when not in use. Refrigerated in an airtight container, this icing can be stored 2 weeks. Rewhip before using. Makes 3 cups.

*Substitute all-vegetable shortening and 1/2 teaspoon Wilton Butter Extract for pure white icing and stiffer consistency.
* *Add 3-4 tablespoons light corn syrup per recipe to thin for icing cake.

You'll need more than one Wilton Sheet Pan to get you through the holidays. High quality anodized aluminum gives you consistent baking success— for cakes, main courses and more. In a variety of sizes for every need.

Happy
Holidays
to
All

Happy
Holidays

CHOCOLATE CHRISTMAS CLASSIC

Wilton 4 Pc. Oval Pan Set (13 x 9 7/8" pan used)
Tips 2, 4, 6, 16, 18, 21, 97
Wilton Christmas Red, Kelly Green, Brown Icing Colors
Wilton Candy Melts ™ — White*
Wilton Cake Board, Fanci-Foil Wrap
Wilton Tree Former Set
Wilton Flower Former Set
Wilton Decorator Brushes
Chocolate buttercream icing *(see p. 42)*
Royal icing *(see p. 39)*
Uncooked spaghetti
Real leaves (do not use poinsettia leaves— lemon, grape and rose leaves work well)

**brand confectionery coating*

Make approximately 14 pine cones using brown royal icing: Wrap waxed paper around tree former. Fold and tape under base. Ice a 2 in. area on end of cone. Pipe tip 97 upright petal at end of cone (turn like a flower nail). Add 2 more upright "center bud" petals, overlapping as you go. Pipe row of 5, then row of 6 petals below bud, turning hand to open petals. Finish with row of 6, then row of 7 petals, turned out until petals lie flat. When dry, remove pine cone from former.

Make approximately 50 pine needles using green royal icing: Break pieces of uncooked spaghetti into desired lengths. Fill decorating bag with green royal icing; use tip 6. Insert a piece of spaghetti into open end of tip, then as you squeeze bag, pull spaghetti out of tip, coating "needle" with icing. Push end into craft block to dry.

Make approximately 30 leaves: Clean and thoroughly dry grape, lemon or rose leaves. Paint melted Candy Melts onto the back of each leaf using a decorator's brush. Set in large flower formers to curve. Let coating set in refrigerator; when completely set, carefully peel off leaves.

To assemble "poinsettias": Place cotton balls under leaves to hold in position. Join leaves together with a small amount of melted candy. Pipe tip 2 multiple dots in flower centers using red royal icing. Let dry.

Ice 2-layer cake top and sides smooth using chocolate buttercream. Using toothpick, dot mark top edge of cake every 3 1/2 in. Pipe tip 18 zigzag garlands 2 in. deep between marks. Pipe tip 16 zigzag garlands approximately 1/2 in. above. Pipe tip 16 fleurs-de-lis between garlands. Edge top with tip 18 reverse shell border, base with tip 21 C-Scrolls outlined with tip 21 reverse C-Scroll border.

Position flowers, pine cones and needles on cake top and side. Attach with dots of icing where necessary. Pipe and overpipe message using melted candy and tip 2; also add tip 2 "berry" dots to highlight pine cone cluster at base. Serves 32.

Individually or collectively, our 4-pc. Oval Pan Set always comes in handy! Build a dramatic holiday tier using all four pans; place your favorite seasonal symbol on top, such as a mini gingerbread house, a tree or a snowman.

Bryan
Angela
Christian
Eileen

The Man Of The Season

Wilton Jolly Santa Pan
Wilton Tips 3, 16, 21
Wilton Black, Copper, Pink, No Taste Red Icing Colors
Wilton Cake Board, Fanci-Foil Wrap
Buttercream Icing *(see p. 42)*
Shoestring Licorice

If filling cake, lightly ice sides before decorating. Outline hat, eyes, mouth, cheeks with tip 3. Pipe tip 3 dots for eyes and mouth. (Flatten with finger dipped in cornstarch.) Cover face, cheeks and mouth with tip 16 stars. Add nose with tip 16 swirl. Pipe tip 21 stripes for moustache and tip 21 reverse shells for beard and eyebrows. Cover hat with tip 21 stars, brim and pompon with tip 233 pull-out strings. Add licorice eyeglasses. Serves 12.

Banana Split Cake

This easy-to-make favorite offers a different flavor, with the same merry look as the cake above.

Wilton Jolly Santa Pan
Marble or chocolate cake mix

Filling
1 envelope (1 1/4 oz.) whipped topping mix
1 pkg. (4 serv.) vanilla instant pudding & pie mix
1 1/2 cups cold milk
3 bananas, sliced
1/4 cup chopped maraschino cherries

Bake and cool cake mix according to package and pan directions. When cool split into two horizontal layers. Blend topping, pudding mix and milk; beat until stiff. Spread on lower half of cooled cake, add bananas and cherries; replace top half and decorate according to above directions.

You can also decorate a wonderful time-saving cake with our Jolly Santa Pan. Just ice smooth and use mini-marshmallows for beard, hat brim and pom-pom. Cinnamon candies make a great hat. Add trims with black shoestring licorice. Faster than you can say "one horse open sleigh," Santa will be ready for the party.

Family Tree

Use your favorite two layer cake recipe or mix and decorate with cookies.

Wilton Treeliteful Pan
Tips 1, 1s, 2, 4, 16, 101, 127D
Christmas Red, Leaf Green, Royal Blue, Golden Yellow, Brown, Black Icing Colors
4-Pc. Gingerbread Family Cookie Cutter Set
Star Cookie Cutters
Cake Board, Fanci-Foil Wrap
Roll-Out Cookie Dough Recipe, see below
Buttercream Icing *(see p. 42)*

Make the cookie recipe below. Out of dough, using smallest of gingerbread family set, cut 14 figures; cut 1 star using smallest star cutter. Bake and cool. Using buttercream icing, decorate figures as follows: Tip 1s eyes, mouths; tip 1 clothes and hair; tip 2 feet. Add tip 101 ribbons with tip 1 names. Outline star with tip 4 strings; fill-in with tip 16 stars. Set cookies aside to dry.

Bake a two-layer cake in Wilton Treeliteful Pan. Cover tree with tip 16 stars. Ice base and bottom of trunk; build-up icing at base so tree skirt flares. Using tip 127D, pipe two ruffles on base. Outline bottom edges of ruffles with tip 2 strings; trim bottom edges with tip 2 pull-out fringe. Add tip 1 dots and snowflakes. Edge top of skirt with tip 4 dots. Add tip 4 dots to tree.

Position figures and star on cake top. Serves 12.

Festive Sugar Cookies

1 cup butter
1 cup sugar
1 large egg
2 teaspoons baking powder
1 teaspoon vanilla
3 cups flour

Preheat oven to 400°. In a large bowl, cream butter and sugar with an electric mixer. Beat in egg and vanilla. Add baking powder and flour, one cup at a time, mixing after each addition. The dough will be very stiff; blend last flour in by hand. Do not chill dough. **Note:** Dough can be tinted with Icing Color. Add small amounts until desired color is reached. **For chocolate cookies:** Stir in 3 ounces melted, unsweetened chocolate (if dough becomes too stiff, add water, a teaspoon at a time).

Divide dough into 2 balls. On a floured surface, roll each ball into a circle approximately 12 inches in diameter and 1/8 in. thick. Dip cutters in flour before each use. Bake cookies on an ungreased cookie sheet on top rack of oven for 6-7 minutes, or until cookies are lightly browned.

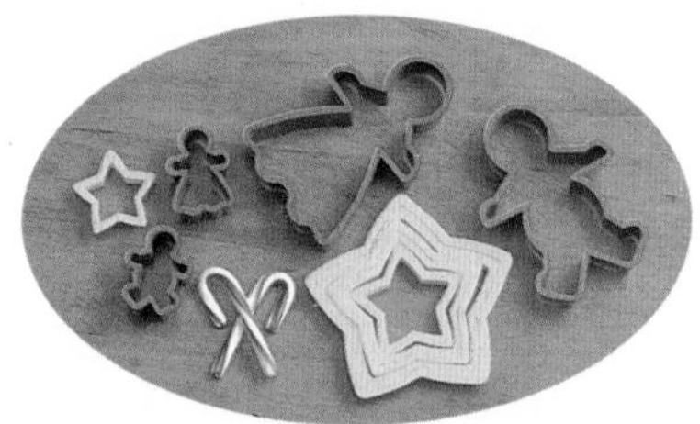

You can do so much with Wilton holiday cookie cutters! Our Gingerbread Family and Star cutter sets are an easy, delicious way to brighten cakes or your party table. Kids will have fun helping add faces, too!

EUREKA, KANS.
GRANDPA
RALPH
NICK
RON
ANN
SUE
DOM

Pretty Packages

Wilton 6, 8, and 10 in. Square Pans
Wilton Tip 6
Rolled Fondant Icing (2 recipes needed)
Wilton Fanci-Foil Wrap, Cake Boards, Dowel Rods
Ribbon
Buttercream Icing *(see p. 42)*

Position 6, 8 and 10 in. 2-layer cakes on individual foil-covered cake boards cut to fit. Ice cakes with buttercream icing. Use 1 fondant recipe to cover 10 in. cake; use second recipe to cover 6 in. and 8 in. cake white.

Using tip 6, add bead bottom borders to cakes. Wrap ribbons around cakes. Secure to bottom board with dots of icing or tape. Position 3 dowels in each cake. Stack cakes. Add top bow. Makes 48 servings.

Rolled Fondant

Fondant is a velvety smooth heavy icing and is best used on a carrot, pound or heavy chocolate cake. Any imperfections will show through fondant, so be sure cake is very smooth when iced with buttercream.

MAKE TWO RECIPES. DO NOT DOUBLE.
2 envelopes gelatin
1/4 cup cold water
1/2 cup warmed Glucose
2 tablespoons solid vegetable shortening
1 tablespoon Glycerine
2 lbs. confectioners sugar
2 - 3 drops liquid food color and flavoring, as desired

In a small saucepan, soften gelatin in water; heat until clear. Add warmed glucose, stir over very low heat until well blended. Add shortening, stir until well blended. Remove from heat, add glycerine, stir until well blended.

If desired, add flavoring and/or food coloring at this time.

Place sugar in a large mixing bowl. Make well in center of confectioners sugar, pour liquid mixture into well. Stir with wooden spoon, then knead with hands until smooth.

Spray work surface and rolling pin with vegetable oil spray, then dust with confectioners sugar and cornstarch. Roll out fondant the diameter of cake plus the height of two sides (for example: 10 in. cake + 4 in. one side + 4 in. other side = 18 in. circle). As you roll, lift and move the fondant to prevent it from sticking to the surface. Gently lift fondant over rolling pin and place over cake.

Smooth and shape fondant on cake, using palm of hand. If large air bubbles are trapped under fondant, prick with a pin and continue to smooth. Trim excess from base. A fondant-covered cake may be kept up to 2 months when tightly wrapped and frozen.

Wilton Square Pans help you bake easy, delicious gifts.
Use them for brownies, bar cookies, cakes and more.
Your baked goods make simple but appreciated holiday treats.

Merry Christmas

BEARING GIFTS

Wilton Santa Bear Pan
Wilton Tips 4, 16, 233
Brown, Kelly Green, Wilton No-Taste Red Icing Colors
Wilton Cake Board, Fanci-Foil Wrap
Buttercream Icing (see p. 42)

With tip 4 outline facial features, paws, gift, ribbon and bow. Pipe in nose, ears and mouth with tip 4 (smooth with finger dipped in cornstarch).

Cover gift and bow with tip 16 stars. Pipe tip 233 pull-out fur on body. Makes 12 servings.

FUDGE FLUFF CAKE

Wilton shaped pans are sized to hold one two layer cake mix or recipe. This dense, moist chocolate cake can be used with any of Wilton's shaped pans.

Wilton Santa Bear Pan
2 cups unsifted flour
2 cups sugar
1 teaspoon baking powder
1 teaspoon baking soda
1/2 teaspoon salt
1 teaspoon vanilla
3/4 cup butter or margarine
1 1/2 cups milk
3 eggs
3 oz. melted unsweetened chocolate

All ingredients should be at room temperature.

Preheat oven to 350°. Grease Santa Bear Pan with vegetable shortening and dust with flour or use a vegetable pan spray.

Place all ingredients in large mixing bowl; blend at low speed; beat 3 minutes at medium speed. Pour batter into prepared pan. Bake 45-50 minutes or until top springs back when touched lightly in center. Cool ten minutes on rack; then turn out of pan and cool before decorating. Makes 12 servings.

Bear hugs all year long! Our Santa Bear brings more than Christmas gifts. Try him at birthdays, too — iced smooth and decorated with candy eyes and mouth, he's a real time-saver.

Marie's Applesauce Cake

Wilton 10 in. Fancy Ring Mold Pan
1 cup butter or margarine, room temperature
2 cups granulated sugar
3 eggs
1 teaspoon baking soda
1/4 cup hot tap water
2 cups sweetened applesauce
4 cups flour
3 tablespoons cocoa
1/2 teaspoon ground cloves
1 teaspoon cinnamon
1/2 teaspoon salt
2 cups raisins or chopped dried apricots
1 cup chopped walnuts
If desired, whipped cream and Tip No. 5

Preheat oven to 350°. Grease and flour Wilton 10 in. Fancy Ring Mold Pan*. Cream butter and sugar in large mixer bowl. Add eggs one at a time, beating between additions. Dissolve soda in hot water, stir into applesauce. In a separate bowl, mix flour and seasonings. Add flour mixture and applesauce alternately to batter. Beat until smooth. Fold in raisins and nuts. Pour into prepared pan. Bake on center rack for 55-65 minutes or until an inserted cake tester comes out clean. Cool 15 minutes on rack, trim top if necessary and invert; cool. Glaze or sprinkle with confectioners sugar. Trim with whipped cream and tip 5 using shell motion. Garnish with marzipan leaves or dried apple slices.

Serve with softly whipped cream.

* Or use Long Loaf Pan, bake for 60-70 minutes.

Everyone loves a homebaked gift, and this cake can be made before the busy holiday season, then frozen for up to 4 months! Use the Wilton 10" Fancy Ring Mold Pan, wrap airtight, then freeze. When the holidays arrive, you'll have plenty of gifts on hand for teachers, newspaper and mail carriers, and for holiday guests! This cake also travels well, so it's the perfect choice to send to out-of-town friends!

Chocolate Angel Cake With Raspberry Sauce

Wilton Angel Food Pan
Wilton Tip 127D
1 Angel Food Cake Mix
3 tablespoons cocoa
2 oz. unsweetened baking chocolate, grated

Prepare Angel Food cake according to package directions, adding cocoa to flour package. Place batter by thirds in ungreased Angel Food pan. Sprinkle grated chocolate between layers. Bake according to package directions; cool.

Whipped Cream

3 cups whipping cream
3 envelopes (2 tablespoons) unflavored gelatin
6 tablespoons water
6 tablespoons confectioners sugar

Soften gelatin in water; heat just until dissolved. Cool but do not allow to set. Gelatin should feel neither hot or cold. Add sugar to cream and whip at medium speed until soft peaks form; add gelatin while beater or processsor is running; whip until of spreading consistency.

Food Processor: Whipping cream in the food processor gives cream a velvety texture and is perfect for icing or piping. Cream does not have the volume of traditional whipped cream. Use metal blade and watch closely; cream whips in a short time.

Place cooled cake rounded side down on 14 in. serving plate. Trim if necessary for cake to set level. Spread a thin layer of whipped cream on top of cake and heavier on sides.

Fill a large (16 in.-18 in.) decorating bag fitted with a #127D large rose tip with whipped cream. Starting from outside edge of cake, pipe three rows of whipped cream ruffles and one ruffle around bottom of cake. Serve with raspberry sauce. Garnish with fresh raspberries or candied cherries and mint leaves.

Raspberry Sauce

1 package frozen raspberries in syrup

Thaw raspberries, process in processor or force through sieve. Processed berries may also be strained to remove seeds. Refrigerate until ready to serve. Makes 12 servings.

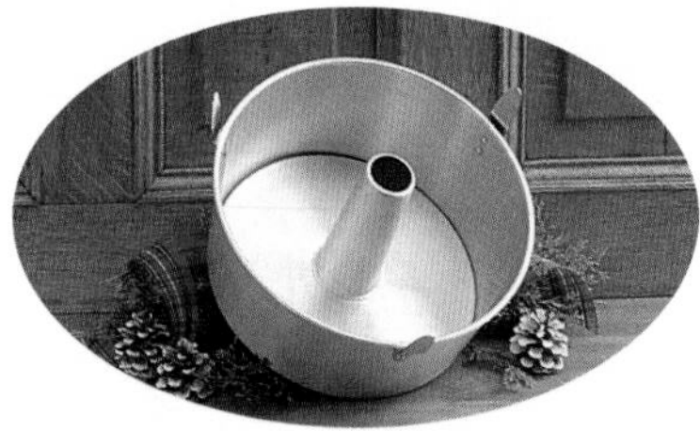

The Wilton Angel Food Pan helps you create high-rising cakes and desserts. Its 4 1/2 in. depth lets you be extra generous during the holidays.

Cranberry Buche De Noel

Yellow Sponge Cake
Even-Bake® Insulated Jelly Roll Pan
5 large eggs
Pinch of salt
1/2 teaspoon cream of tartar
1/2 cup sifted granulated sugar
3/4 cup sifted cake flour
3/4 teaspoon vanilla

Preheat oven to 400°. Line 10 1/2 in. x 15 1/2 in. jelly roll pan with waxed or parchment paper; lightly grease paper. Separate eggs; beat yolks 1 minute. Add pinch of salt to egg whites, beat until foamy. Add cream of tartar and continue beating whites until they cling to bottom and sides of bowl, beat 1 minute longer. Fold beaten egg yolks into egg whites gently but quickly, then fold (do not stir) in sugar, flour and vanilla.

Pour batter into pan, spreading evenly from center out. Tap pan several times on table to break any air bubbles. Bake in center of oven 13-15 minutes. Loosen sides. Turn out of pan onto clean kitchen towel sprinkled with 1 tablespoon granulated sugar. Remove waxed paper; roll cake from long side and let cool, seam side down. Makes 10 servings.

Filling
1 (12 oz.) package fresh cranberries
1 cup sugar
1 tablespoon orange liqueur
1 packet (2 teaspoons) unflavored gelatin
2 tablespoons cold water
8 oz. softened cream cheese in 1 in. chunks
1 cup whipping cream
Whipped Cream Recipe, p. 56
Meringue Recipe, p. 61

NOTE: *1 cup fresh cranberries and 1 cup sugar may be replaced with 1 (16 oz.) can whole cranberry sauce. In a small saucepan, break sauce apart and heat. Proceed with remaining recipe directions.*

Heat, on range top or microwave, cranberries and sugar until they come to a boil and most of the berries have broken. On range top, start on low heat until sugar dissolves; do not add water; add orange liqueur; cool slightly. Soften gelatin in cold water; heat until liquid and clear. Add gelatin and cranberry mixture to food processor and process until smooth. Cool; add cream cheese and process until smooth (or beat with mixer until smooth). Whip cream until soft peaks form; fold into cranberry mixture. Unroll cake and spread filling to within 1 in. of ends. Re-roll and place seam side down.

Cut two 1 in. slices at an angle from each end, reserve. Place roll on serving plate seam side down.

Use whipped cream recipe on page 56. Cover with whipped cream; score with fork or skewer. Place two pieces on roll for ends of branches. Cover with whipped cream. Refrigerate before cutting.

Garnish with cranberries and meringue mushrooms. To make mushrooms, use meringue recipe, p. 61. Fill bag fitted with tip 1A with meringue. Pipe dot mushroom "caps" and line "stems" on paper-lined cookie sheet. Bake at 225° for 30-40 minutes or until stems are crisp and caps are crisp on top. Lift stems from paper and cool. Turn caps over, press in underneath and bake 15 minutes longer or until dry. Attach stems to caps with melted Candy Melts™ or chocolate.

The Wilton Even-Bake® Insulated Jelly Roll Pan bakes without hot spots, producing a uniformly baked, perfectly browned cake. It's the secret to rolling the Buche De Noel without breaking it!

Christmas Meringue

Dessert must be served immediately after baking,
but can be frozen decorated with meringue until ready to bake.

Wilton 8 in. Round Pan
Wilton Wonder Mold Pan
1/2 gallon vanilla ice cream
1 pint cherry ice cream
1 pint pistachio ice cream
1 baked 8 in. round brownie, 1-1 1/2 in. high

Soften ice cream 15-30 seconds on high in microwave or 10-15 minutes at room temperature. Place each flavor in separate bowls. Stir each until smooth but not melted. Line Wonder Mold with plastic wrap. (Do not use core.) Make a shell of vanilla ice cream by pressing and smoothing against sides of mold with a spoon, leave approximately 1 in. space at top. Make next layer of cherry. Fill center with pistachio, smooth top. (If ice cream is too soft to form layers return briefly to freezer.) Place brownie on top and press until even with top of Wonder Mold. Cover with foil and freeze overnight or up to one week.

Unmold ice cream, remove plastic wrap. Place on ovenproof serving tray or baking pan which can be placed on serving tray. Return to freezer while preparing meringue. Ice cream must be frozen hard when baked. If piping meringue onto ice cream takes more than 5 minutes, return dessert to freezer before baking.

Meringue
6 tablespoons Wilton Meringue Powder
3/4 cup cold water
1 1/4 cups granulated sugar

Place oven rack on lowest position and preheat oven to 450°. Combine meringue powder, water and one-half the sugar in a large mixer bowl. Whip at high speed for five minutes. Gradually add remaining sugar and continue whipping for 5 minutes or until stiff peaks form.

Spread thin layer of meringue over ice cream mold, be sure to cover surface. Fill large pastry bag fitted with tip 1A with meringue. Pipe large dots over thin meringue layer.

Place in pre-heated oven and bake until lightly browned, approximately 5-6 minutes. Serve immediately. 12 servings.

The Wilton Wonder Mold is great for year-round celebrations. This recipe can be used for every holiday by substituting ice cream flavors—use strawberry and chocolate for Valentine's Day; mint for St. Patrick's Day; strawberry, vanilla and blueberry for the 4th of July!

Cherry Christmas Tart

Pastry
Wilton Treeliteful Pan
Wilton 6-pc. Nesting Star Cookie Cutter Set
2 1/4 cups flour
1/8 teaspoon salt
3/4 cup butter, cold, cut into chunks
1 egg
5-6 tablespoons cold water

In a large food processor bowl fitted with a metal blade, cut butter into flour and salt, until it resembles coarse meal. Add egg and water, one tablespoon at a time, until pastry forms into a ball. Do not over mix or over process. Form into a flat disk and refrigerate one hour. Roll out into approximately 5 x 14 x 10 in. tree shape. Place pan top side down on dough. Using pan as pattern, cut about 3/4 in. from edge of pan. Fold pastry and place in pan. Dough should not come up to top edge of pan. To make rope trim: cut long strips of dough approximately 1/4 in. wide. Twist together. Brush top edge of pastry with water. Place twist on edge and press lightly. Prick bottom of pastry with fork. Cut stars from excess pastry, place on cookie sheet and prick with fork. Bake at 425° for 5-15 minutes or until browned. If desired, brush pastry with an egg wash (1 tablespoon water and one egg yolk) the last 5-10 minutes of baking time. Do not brush egg wash on pan or pastry will stick.

Cool pastry 10 minutes in pan and remove to serving plate. Let cool completely before filling.

NOTE: One 15 oz. package of refrigerated ready rolled pie crust may be substituted. Overlap and piece dough by brushing edges with water. Bake according to package directions. Pastry shell may be less uniform on the edges than when made with the recipe.

Filling
6 tablespoons lemon juice
1 (8 oz.) package cream cheese, slightly softened
1 (14 oz.) can sweetened condensed milk, not evaporated
1 tablespoon orange liqueur, optional
1 (26 oz.) can cherry pie filling

Place all ingredients, except pie filling, in food processor or large mixer bowl. Process, or beat, until smooth. Pour into prepared crust. Refrigerate one hour or until firm. Top with cherry pie filling. Tart may be refrigerated 3-4 hours before serving. Place stars and tree base on tart just before serving. Cheese filling may be made one day before serving, refrigerate and add to baked crust. Proceed as above. Makes 8 servings.

You can create a shimmering Christmas tree with the Treeliteful Pan. Mold a layer of lime gelatin below a layer of cherry gelatin and cream cheese, then let it set in the refrigerator. Add several maraschino cherries to lime gelatin for "bulbs" before chilling.

Cookies & Brownies

Apricot Bars

Wilton 12 x 18 in. Jelly Roll Pan
1 $^1/_2$ cups (12 oz) dried apricots
2 $^2/_3$ cups flour, divided
$^1/_2$ cup sugar
$^1/_4$ cup brown sugar
1 cup butter or margarine, softened
2 cups chopped walnuts
1 teaspoon baking powder
$^1/_2$ teaspoon salt
4 eggs, slightly beaten
2 cups brown sugar, firmly packed
1 teaspoon vanilla

Cook apricots in boiling water for 10 minutes; drain. Cool and cut into small pieces. Set aside.

Combine 2 cups flour, sugars, butter or margarine and 1 cup walnuts; mix until crumbly. Press $^2/_3$ of crumb mixture into ungreased 12 x 18 in. jelly roll pan. Bake in 350^0 oven 10 minutes or until golden brown. In a small bowl mix $^2/_3$ cup flour, baking powder, salt and slightly beaten eggs. Add brown sugar and mix well. Add vanilla. Mix in chopped apricots and remaining walnuts. Spread over baked crust. Sprinkle reserved $^1/_3$ crumb mixture evenly on top. Bake additional 25-30 minutes. Cool and cut into bars. Decorate with thinned buttercream icing if desired. Store at cool room temperature separated by waxed paper for two weeks or freeze for up to two months. Makes 40 1 $^1/_2$ x 3 in. bars.

Chocolate Streusel Bars

Wilton 12 x 18 in. Jelly Roll Pan

Crust:

3 $^1/_4$ cups flour, divided
1 cup finely chopped pecans
$^3/_4$ cup cocoa
1 $^1/_2$ cups butter, softened
1 $^1/_2$ cups confectioners sugar

Filling:

2 (8 oz) pkgs. cream cheese, softened
2 eggs
2 (14 oz) cans sweetened condensed milk, not evaporated
2 teaspoons vanilla extract

Preheat oven to 350^0. In a bowl combine 3 cups flour, pecans and cocoa, set aside. In a large mixing bowl, cream butter and sugar until light and fluffy. Add flour mixture and beat just until well blended. Do not overbeat. Press $^2/_3$ of mixture onto bottom of ungreased 12 x 18 in. jelly roll pan. Stir remaining $^1/_4$ cup flour into reserved crust mixture and save for streusel topping. Bake crust 10 minutes.

In a large mixing bowl beat softened cream cheese until fluffy, add eggs, beating well after each addition. Slowly add sweetened condensed milk and vanilla, mix until smooth. Pour into prebaked crust. Sprinkle streusel topping evenly over cheese mixture. Bake 30 minutes. Cool then chill and cut into bars. Store covered in refrigerator. Makes 40 1 $^1/_2$ x 3 in. bars.

Our 12 x 18 in. Jelly Roll Pan makes it easy to bake dozens of bar cookies for holiday giving.
Neighbors will welcome freshly-baked brownies, fruitbars and even fudge.
Count on Wilton to help you share the warmth of the season.

Pecan Tassies

Pastry

Wilton Mini Muffin Pan
1/2 cup (1 stick) butter, softened
1 (3 oz) package cream cheese, room temperature
1 cup flour

Preheat oven to 350°. In a small bowl blend butter and cream cheese with mixer, add flour, mix until a soft dough forms. Do not overmix; refrigerate pastry one hour. Divide into 30 walnut sized balls. Use tart tamper to form dough in mini-muffin cups, trim excess dough off top edge. Fill pastry with pecan filling. Bake 20-25 minutes or until pastry is light brown. Cool 5 minutes, remove from pan to cool. Store at room temperature in one layer in flat container for up to one week or freeze for two months.

Filling

1 1/2 cups brown sugar
2 tablespoons melted butter
2 eggs, slightly beaten
1/4 teaspoon vanilla
pinch of salt
1/2 cup chopped pecans

In a small bowl add melted butter to brown sugar, mix. Add eggs, vanilla and salt, stir until blended. Mix in pecans. Makes 2 1/2 dozen.

Mini Chocolate Cherry Tarts

Pastry Crust

Wilton Mini Muffin Pan
1 1/2 cups flour
1/3 cup sugar
1/4 cup unsweetened cocoa
1/2 cup butter or margarine
1 tablespoon water

Preheat oven to 350°F. In a small bowl combine flour, sugar and cocoa. Cut in margarine or butter until pieces are the size of small peas. Sprinkle with water, tossing until moistened. Form into 1 in. diameter log. Divide pastry into 30 balls. Place in ungreased mini-muffin pan; press dough evenly, using tart tamper. Top with cream cheese mixture. Bake in a 350° oven for 15-20 minutes or until done. Remove from pans; cool completely. Top each with teaspoon of cherry pie filling.

Cream Cheese Mixture

2 (8 oz.) pkgs. cream cheese
1 cup sugar
2 eggs
2 teaspoons vanilla

Beat cream cheese until light and creamy, gradually add sugar, mix well. Add eggs 1 at a time, mixing well after each addition. Stir in vanilla. Makes 2 1/2 dozen.

Our Mini Muffin Pan is the perfect size for holiday brunches. Serve baskets of assorted muffin flavors — poppyseed, lemon, corn, blueberry — along with flavored cream cheese and butter for an easy Christmas morning breakfast.

Cream Cheese Spritz

Wilton Spritz Cookie Press
1 cup butter, softened
1 (3 oz.) package cream cheese, softened
1 cup sugar
1 egg yolk
1 teaspoon vanilla extract
1 teaspoon grated lemon peel
2 1/2 cups flour
1/2 teaspoon salt

Preheat oven to 350°F. Cream butter and cream cheese together. Add sugar and mix well until light and fluffy. Add egg yolk, vanilla and lemon peel. Mix well. Gradually add flour and salt to cream mixture. Shape dough in small logs and place in Wilton cookie press. Press cookies onto cool ungreased cookie sheet.

Bake 12-15 minutes or until lightly browned.

To make green trees add a small amount of Leaf Green paste color to dough before shaping into logs. To make red/white cookies, add Wilton Red to one half dough. Shape red and plain dough separately into narrow logs; place together into Wilton Spritz Cookie Press. Follow above instructions for shaping.

Store in an airtight container at cool room temperature for several weeks or freeze for two months. Makes 4 dozen cookies.

Chocolate Spritz

Wilton Spritz Cookie Press
1 1/4 cups butter or margarine
3/4 cup sugar
2/3 cup brown sugar
2 large eggs
3 1/4 cups flour
3/4 cup cocoa
1/2 teaspoon baking soda
1/4 teaspoon salt
Wilton vanilla Candy Melts™ or buttercream icing *(see p. 42)*

Preheat oven to 375°. In a large mixing bowl cream butter and sugars at medium high speed until light and fluffy. Add eggs, one at a time, beating well after each addition. Sift together flour, cocoa, soda and salt. Add flour mixture gradually and beat well. Shape dough into small log and place in cookie press. Press cookies onto cool ungreased cookie sheets. Bake at 375° for 10-12 minutes. Remove from sheet and cool. Decorate by dipping into melted vanilla Candy Melts™ brand confectionery coating and dipping in chocolate sprinkles or sandwich with buttercream icing.

Store in an airtight container at cool room temperature for several weeks or freeze for two months. Makes 5 dozen cookies.

The Wilton Spritz Cookie Press makes it easy to create dozens of holiday shapes in minutes. Make your celebration more fun by matching flavor to cookie color. Add a touch of mint to green cookies, cherry to red, orange to orange with drops of flavor extract for a great party surprise.

SUGAR COOKIES

Wilton 10-pc. Christmas Cookie Cutter Collection
Wilton 4-pc. Christmas Favorites Cookie Cutter Set
Wilton Tips 2,12, 233, 347
Wilton Color Flow Mix
Wilton Edible Glitter
1/2 cup butter
1 cup sugar
1 egg
1 teaspoon baking powder
1 3/4 cups flour
1 tablespoon milk
1/2 teaspoon vanilla
1/4 teaspoon salt
Ground chocolate or cocoa powder
Silver dragees
Jelly or packaged lemon curd, if desired

Preheat oven to 375°F. Cream butter and sugar, add egg and mix. Add remaining ingredients and mix until smooth. Refrigerate 2 hours. Roll out 1/8 in. thick on lightly floured surface, dip cutter in flour before each use. Place on ungreased cookie sheet. Bake 12-15 minutes or until browned. Remove from sheet and cool.

Decorate with buttercream icing, or for jewel trees: roll dough on cookie sheet, 1/16 in. thick; cut tree shapes. Make cutouts with tip 12 on one half of the trees. Bake 8-10 minutes, remove from pan and cool. Spread jelly or lemon curd on plain tree, top with cut out tree. Dust with confectioners sugar. For Bear, Boots and Reindeer, make color flow according to directions on can and tint. Paint cookies and let dry. Dust Reindeer with ground chocolate or cocoa powder. Pipe tip 2 eyes, add silver dragees. Pipe tip 2 zigzag collar and hooves; tip 347 leaves and tip 2 dot berries. Cover boots with tip 2 dots and tip 233 pull-out fur cuff. Trim bears with edible glitter, tip 2 outline clothes, tip 2 dot buttons eyes and nose. Add tip 233 fur on ears, tip 347 leaves and tip 2 berries. Makes 1 dozen large cookies.

PEANUT BUTTER CUTOUTS

Wilton 4-pc. Christmas Favorites Cookie Cutter Set
1 cup solid vegetable shortening
1 cup peanut butter
1 cup granulated sugar
1 cup packed brown sugar
2 eggs
1 teaspoon vanilla
3 cups flour
1 teaspoon baking soda
Dash salt

Preheat oven to 350°. In a large mixing bowl cream together shortening and peanut butter. Gradually add sugars, blending well. Add eggs, one at a time, beating until smooth. Add vanilla. Set aside. Combine flour, baking soda and salt. Stir into peanut butter mixture. Divide dough into two parts. Roll on lightly floured surface, to approximately 1/4 in. To make cookies with closed cutter, roll dough just slightly less than depth of cutter. Dip cutter in flour before each cut. With spatula place cookies on ungreased cookie sheet. Bake 8-10 minutes or until lightly browned. Remove from sheets and cool. Store in tightly covered container at cool room temperature for several weeks or freeze for up to two months. Makes 3 dozen medium size cookies.

Great shapes for merry things to come! Holiday cutters galore for fun, delicious roll-out cookies and more... Our holiday cutters come in many shapes and sizes so there's something for everyone — super for craft projects, too!

THUMBPRINT COOKIES

Even-Bake ® Cookie Sheet
1/2 cup butter or margarine, softened
1/4 cup brown sugar
1 egg, separated
1/2 teaspoon vanilla
1 cup flour
1/4 teaspoon salt
3/4 cup finely chopped walnuts
Jelly or candied fruit, if desired

Preheat oven to 350°. In a medium mixing bowl cream butter or margarine with brown sugar until light and fluffy. Add egg yolk and vanilla. Mix well. Toss flour and salt together, add to creamed mixture. Mix until ingredients form a ball.

In a shallow dish beat egg white slightly. Shape dough into 1 1/2 in. balls. Roll in egg whites, then in nuts. Place on cookie sheet; bake 5 minutes, then make thumb impression and bake additional 7-10 minutes. Remove from cookie sheet, cool. Fill with jelly or candied fruit. Dust with confectioners sugar if desired.

Store cookies in an airtight container several weeks or freeze for two months. Do not add jelly or dust with sugar if you plan to store. Makes 2 dozen.

CHOCOLATE MELTS

Even-Bake ® Cookie Sheet
1 cup butter, softened
1/2 cup sugar
1 egg, separated
1/2 teaspoon vanilla
1 oz. unsweetened chocolate, melted
2 cups flour
1/4 teaspoon salt
1 cup chopped nuts

Preheat oven to 350°. In a medium mixing bowl beat butter, sugar, egg yolk, vanilla and melted chocolate until light and fluffy. Add flour and salt. Mix well. Roll dough into balls about the size of walnuts. Dip into slightly beaten egg white and then in chopped nuts. Place on ungreased cookie sheet and press thumb in center of each. Bake at 350° for 12-15 minutes. Remove from cookie sheet and cool. Fill baked thumbprints with icing, candied fruit, jelly or melted chocolate.

Cookies can be stored tightly covered at room temperature for several weeks or frozen for two months. If stored, do not fill until ready to serve. Makes 4 dozen.

Browned, not burnt, cookies every time with an Even-Bake ® Insulated Cookie Sheet. Perfect for baked goods rich in butter that may burn easily — luscious cookies, flaky biscuits, fancy pastries. Totally immersible and dishwasher-safe for quick, easy clean-up, too! Selected by Jeff Smith, the Frugal Gourmet ™.

Christmas Shortbread

Wilton Mini Bears Pan
Even Bake® Insulated 8 in. Round Pan
1 cup butter
3/4 cup sugar
1 teaspoon vanilla
2 1/2 cups flour

In a medium mixing bowl cream butter, sugar and vanilla. Add flour and mix until dough is smooth. Chill dough one hour.

Preheat oven to 300°. For round shortbreads: Divide dough in half, press into two ungreased 8" round pans. Make designs by scoring with spatula and imprinting with small cookie cutters and the end of a pastry tube. For bear shortbreads: Divide dough into twelve equal parts. Press in ungreased mini bear pan. Bake rounds 25-30 minutes; bears 20-25 minutes or until very lightly browned. Cool 10 minutes in pans and remove shortbread to cool. Shortbread can be stored in an airtight container at room temperature for several weeks or frozen for two months. Cut rounds into wedges with a sharp knife.

Makes two 8 in. rounds or 12 Mini-Bears.

Chunky Apple Cookies

Even Bake® Insulated Cookie Sheet
1 1/2 cups flour
1 teaspoon baking powder
1/2 teaspoon salt
1 teaspoon cinnamon
1/2 teaspoon nutmeg
3/4 cup solid vegetable shortening or softened butter
1 cup brown sugar
1 egg
1 cup diced unpeeled apples
1 1/2 cups oatmeal, not instant
1/2 cup chopped nuts
1/2 cup raisins

Preheat oven to 350°. In large mixing bowl, mix first 8 ingredients until smooth. Fold in apples, oats, nuts and raisins. Drop by tablespoon on cookie sheet. Bake 20 minutes. Remove from sheet and cool. Cookies are best when placed in an airtight container as soon as cool.

Can be stored at cool room temperature for several weeks or frozen for two months.

Makes 5 dozen cookies.

Bears can take center table at any occasion with our Mini Bear Pan — "Bear" rolls, muffins, brownies, cakes, cookies and gelatin are fun and easy!

Blonde Brownie Snowmen

Wilton Mini-Snowman Pan
Wilton Tips 2, 3, 47, 349
2 cups brown sugar
1 cup butter or margarine, melted
4 eggs
2 cups flour
1/2 teaspoon baking powder
2 teaspoons vanilla
2 cups chopped walnuts

Preheat oven to 350°F. In mixing bowl, combine sugar and melted butter. Add eggs one at a time to sugar mixture, mixing between additions. Sift flour and baking powder together. Combine with sugar mixture. Add vanilla and nuts. Blend well. Generously spray each Mini-Snowman cavity with non-stick vegetable spray. Bake 20-25 minutes, let cool 10 minutes; remove from pan. Do not let brownies set in pan more than 10 minutes or they will be difficult to remove. Dust with confectioners sugar. Pipe scarf with tip 47. Eyes and buttons with tip 3 dots. Hat trim with tip 349 leaves and tip 2 dot berries.

Brownies may also be baked in an 8 in. square pan. Spray pan with vegetable spray; bake 20-25 minutes. Cool before cutting. It is easier to cut brownies in perfect squares if pan is lined with foil before baking. Remove foil and brownies from pan when cool. Cut with long bladed knife. To freeze, leave in one piece, wrap airtight. Remove, thaw and cut when ready to serve. Makes 9 Snowmen.

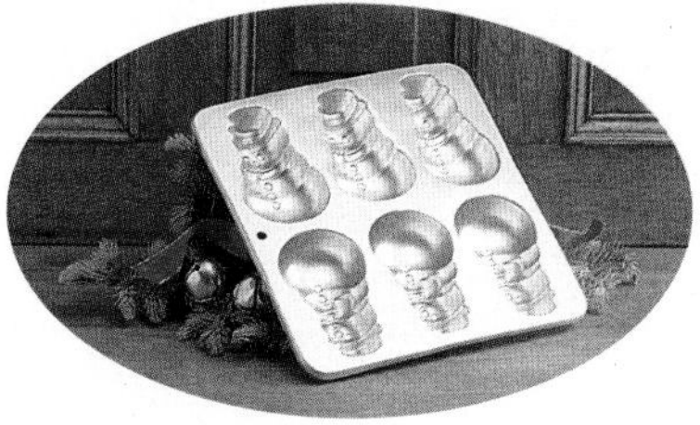

Our Mini-Snowman Pan creates dozens of lovable cakes. Decorate with candy and you're ready for fun!
For a pretty picture in the "snow"—Place a stencil or doily on cake or serving dish.
Cover with sifted confectioners sugar. Remove carefully.

Chocolate Brownies

Even-Bake® Insulated 7 x 11 in. Pan
Wilton Mini-Christmas Tree Pan
Wilton Tips 2, 15
2 squares unsweetened chocolate, melted
3/4 cup butter, melted
1 1/2 cups sugar
2 eggs, slightly beaten
1/8 teaspoon salt
1 cup flour
1 teaspoon vanilla
1 cup chopped nuts

Preheat oven to 350°F. In a small heavy sauce pan or microwave-safe bowl, melt chocolate and butter together on low heat, stir until blended. Place sugar in mixing bowl, add chocolate mixture, mix. Add eggs, blend. Toss salt and flour together in a separate bowl. Add flour, nuts and vanilla to mixture, stir until all flour is mixed in. Spray Mini Christmas Tree or 7 x 11 in. pan liberally with vegetable spray. Fill pans 2/3 full. Bake 20 minutes. Cool 10 minutes in pan; release. For squares, cool in pan. Cut into squares. Decorate squares with candy canes and bows. Fit a bag with star tip 15. Place red icing on one side of bag and white on other. Pipe candy canes. Make bows with tip 2. To make bow, hold bag at a 45° angle to surface. While squeezing, move the tip up and around to the starting point and continue around, making a second loop on the left. The two loops should form a figure 8. Still holding bag in the same position return to the center and squeeze out two streamers. Decorate trees with tip 15 stars; tip 2 dots and swags. Note instructions with Blonde Brownies for cutting and freezing. Makes 6 Trees.

When is a brownie more than a brownie? When it's baked and decorated in the Christmas spirit, using Wilton Mini Christmas Tree and 7 x 11 in. pans and Wilton tips. Same delicious taste as your traditional brownie, but adorned with our suggested trimmings, it becomes a special holiday treat!

THIS IS
CHRIS' PLACE

Gingerbread
& Crafts

A Holiday Happening

Wilton Gingerbread House Kit
Gingerbread Recipe (included in kit)
Wilton Tips 3, 16 (included in kit)
3 16 in. Round Cake Boards (for base)
1 10 in. Round Cake Board (for skating pond)
Royal Icing (page 39)
Silver Foil
Assorted Candy Trims—small candy canes, sugar coated discs and sticks, jelly candies, cinnamon dots, spearmint leaves, red string licorice, gum squares, gum drops

Wrap triple-stacked 16 in. round cake boards with silver foil for sturdy base. Make gingerbread following recipe included with kit. Cut pieces using patterns for the basic house with arched door and square windows. Also cut these additional pieces:
2 sleds using arched door pattern and 1 sled using arched window pattern, and 5 people. Bake, cool, and assemble.

Ice roof, position disc candies; trim roof, windows, door, edge seams with tip 16 zigzags. Position cinnamon dots along eaves, candy sticks and half discs for windows, add candy canes along roof and edge seams. Decorate door with jelly ring wreath attached with icing, attach door; position trees on outside walls of house using spearmint leaves, cinnamon dots and dots of icing. Position other candies as desired. Generously ice base, add path in front of door. Decorate sleds using tip 16, candy canes, string licorice, and gingerbread people. For sitting sledder, cut cookie in half. Decorate people using tip 3 for outlines and facial features, and tip 16 stars for clothing. Trim with candies and candy canes. Snowman is covered with tip 16 stars, trimmed with candy. Cover gum drops with tip 3 strings to resemble wrapped gifts; position on sled.

For pond: Cover small board with silver foil, fluff icing around edge with spatula, to resemble snow.

Position sleds and people around house and pond.

The Wilton Gingerbread House Kit includes what you need to build a beautiful holiday house! You get complete instructions for 4 unique designs; plus patterns, cutters, decorating tips, bags, recipes for icing and Grandma's Gingerbread. . .even tips on keeping your gingerbread construction for years to come!

GINGERBREAD COOKIES

Delicious cookies that make delightful ornaments. It's easy to bake and decorate all the shapes Wilton makes (and we have many more than we show here). It's just what you need to add a new twist to this year's mantle or tree. And while they're baking, the whole house will smell like Christmas!

Wilton Giant Gingerbread Boy Cookie Cutters
Wilton Perimeter Locomotive Engine, Roller Skate, Sailboat, Teddy Bear, Rocking Horse Cookie Cutters
8 cups flour
1 cup brown sugar
1 1/4 cup molasses
3 eggs
1 cup butter, room temperature
1 teaspoon soda
1 teaspoon salt
1 teaspoon allspice
1 teaspoon cloves
1 teaspoon cinnamon
1 teaspoon ginger

Preheat oven to 375°. Reserve 5 cups flour. Mix 3 cups flour and remaining ingredients in a large mixing bowl at low speed until blended. Scrape bowl often. Increase speed to medium and beat two minutes, or until very smooth. Reduce speed to low; add remaining flour 1 cup at a time until dough is very stiff. If you are using a small mixer the last flour may need to be stirred or kneaded by hand. Follow directions below for shaping cookies. Wrap pieces of dough with plastic wrap to keep from drying. Dough may be stored in refrigerator and brought to room temperature before rolling. Store cookies 2-3 weeks. Baked gingerbread readily absorbs moisture. Store in a cool dry place. If you live in a high humidity area, back large cookies with stiff paperboard attached with icing.

For Small Cookies: Divide dough into three pieces. Roll each piece into a circle approximately 12 in. diameter, 1/8 in. thick. Dip cutters in flour before cutting. Place cookies on ungreased cookie sheet. Use the end of round pastry tips, small pieces of dough and the end of a rounded spatula to make designs and features on cookie shapes. For skate ties cut holes with tip 10 round and with tip 5 for yarn ties. Bake 8-10 minutes or until lightly browned, remove to rack to cool. Makes 6-7 dozen small cookies.

For Large Cookies: Divide dough into 4 pieces. To make handling large cookies easier roll dough directly on cookie sheet, approximately 9 x 16 x 1/4 in. Dip cutters in flour and cut. Remove excess dough. Make features with pastry tips. For ribbon tie cut two holes side by side at neck. Bake 10-15 minutes or until lightly browned. Let cool on sheet for 2-3 minutes. Remove carefully with large spatula. Cool on rack. When cool, thread ribbon through neck and tie. Makes 7-10 large gingerbread boys.

Wilton cutters come in all shapes and sizes to make your holiday more fun. And these easy to handle plastic cutters won't harm little fingers.

NORTH
POLE

Santa's Toy Shop

Wilton Gingerbread House Kit
Wilton Tips 1, 2, 3, 5, 8, 8B, 32, 47, 352
Wilton Kelly Green, Wilton No-Taste Red, Black, Brown, Copper, Royal Blue, Lemon Yellow Icing Colors
Wilton Tree Former Set
Wilton Edible Glitter
Wilton Appaloosa Rocking Horse Set
Wilton Train Cake Top Set
Wilton 4-Pc. Darling Dolls Set
Wilton 4-Pc. Party Teddy Bear Candles Set
Wilton Derby Clowns Set
Wilton Message Cake Pick
Wilton Cake Board, Fanci-Foil Wrap
Royal Icing Recipe (page 39)
Gingerbread Recipe (in kit)
Ice cream cake cups
Large marshmallows
Black string licorice
7-8 wrapped candy pieces
Silver dragees
Blue plastic wrap

Follow gingerbread recipe, using cutting, constructing and baking instructions included in kit with these variations: Make 3 walls and 2 dormers; using the steeple base as a pattern, cut 3 windows.

Divide the dough cut-out from one window in half for the 2 shelves.

Assemble all pieces, position on foil-covered 20 x 15 in. oval board. Add and fluff icing with spatula for snow, sprinkle with edible glitter.

Outline all wall and dormer edges front and back with tip 32. Outline windows and shelves with tip 47, add tip 8 dots at corners of windows.

Pipe wreaths above each window using tip 352. Add tip 2 berry trim. Attach plastic wrap pieces cut slightly larger than window size to outside with icing. Add snowflakes with tip 1; pipe tip 8 snowdrifts and icicles.

For trees: Cover waxed-paper-wrapped Tree Formers with tip 352 pull-out leaves and snow.
For sign: Use tip 3 and add snow and message to Message Cake Pick.
For paint cans: Place licorice piece in marshmallow, add tip 2 "paint".
For elves: Pipe tip 8B bodies, arms and legs, either sitting in Ice Cream Cake Cups which have top half removed on one side; or sitting upright. Add tip 352 pull-out collar. Trim with silver dragees at collar points. Edge top of cones with tip 2 zigzags. Remove plastic collars from clown picks, insert into bodies. Pipe tip 3 white over existing eye areas; add tip 3 eyebrows and beards, noses and mouths. Add tip 2 pupils. Add tip 32 hat with tip 3 fur trim. Add tip 5 hands and tip 8 shoes and trim with tip 3 fur; trim shoes with silver dragees.

Note: Position toys as soon as piping is finished; if toy or list is held in lap, position before piping arms and hands. Make a hammer and paint brushes using black licorice and tip 3. Position in elves' hands. Let all dry.

Attach trees and sign to snow-covered ground with dots of icing. Position Darling Dolls atop stacked wrapped candy pieces at outside windows. Place elves, trains, rocking horses, teddy bears, and paint cans at desired positions in toy shop.

Wilton candles and cake toppers add the perfect finishing touches to your holiday creations. There are so many styles to choose from — mix and match them as we have done here, to create your own Christmas scene.

Cinnamon Molds

Use these fragrant little yuletide characters to hang on the tree, or as package or wreath decorations.

Wilton Candy Molds (Christmas I, Christmas II, Christmas Classics Sets I & II, Christmas Trees)
1/4 cup applesauce
1/2 cup cinnamon or cinnamon/nutmeg mixture
Ribbon
Place cards
Hot glue gun

Put both ingredients in small bowl. Mix until moistened. Mixture will be crumbly. Press into candy molds; let dry approximately 1 hour, remove from molds and dry at least overnight.

After drying, place a spot of glue on the back, then press ribbon onto glue. Be careful not to burn fingers on hot glue. Add ribbons to gift packages, windows, Christmas trees, etc. Or glue characters directly onto gift packages, placecards, nametags.

To make a napkin ring, fold napkin and wrap with a wide ribbon, gluing ribbon at back. Glue on a cinnamon character.

Lollipops also make great package decorations. Choose your favorite shapes from the wide variety of Wilton Christmas Candy Molds, mold lollipops using Candy Melts™ brand confectionery coating in holiday colors and lollipop sticks. Then tie the pops right onto your gifts!

Grandpa
Aunt Marie

WELCOME TO
KATHY'S PLACE

Holiday Sweatshirt

It's easy and fun to make these Christmas keepsakes. Great gifts that will be brought out every holiday season.

Wilton Giant Tree and Giant Gingerbread Boy Cookie Cutters
Sweatshirt
Fabric Paints, various colors
Pencil

Flatten sweatshirt on work surface. Position Giant Gingerbread Boy cutter in center; trace with pencil. Place and trace Giant Tree cutters, one at a time, on either side of Boy tracing.

Outline Gingerbread Boy with paint, add dot border at inner edge of outline. Add nose at center of face area, then add eyes and mouth. Add three "button" dots, then dot borders around button. Outline trees and fill in with random continuous zigzags. Add red "ornaments". Follow specific paint instructions for drying and laundering.

Personalized Placemats

Wilton Nesting Bear Cookie Cutters
Wilton Make-A-Message Pattern Press Kit
Placemat
Fabric Paints, various colors
Pencil
Chalk or Cinnamon

Flatten placemat on work surface. Place medium size bear cutter in center, slightly more toward bottom of mat. Trace with pencil. Place and trace large bears, one at a time, on either side of small bear tracing. Outline bears with paint, adding faces, buttons and bows.

Create words of message on Make-A-Message tool. Rub edges of letters with chalk or cinnamon and press into position to leave an impression. Repeat for other words of message. Outline message with paint.

Make decorative borders with dots of paint. Follow specific paint instructions for drying and laundering.

Wilton Giant Cutters make a big hit with kids. There's more space to decorate—with colored cookie dough, sprinkles, raisins and candies. Give everyone at the party an individual Gingerbread Boy, with name and wardrobe traced in icing!

Santa Plaque

Wilton Jolly Santa Pan
Wilton Candy Molds
liquid detergent
1 1/2 lbs. plaster of paris
water
fine sandpaper
florist wire
acrylic paints
paper towels
wreath, greens and ribbon

To prepare plaster casting: squirt about 1 tablespoon liquid detergent into bottom of Jolly Santa Pan. Rub with fingers across bottom surface of pan and half way up sides. For candy molds, rub a dab of detergent into each mold. With a paper towel, wipe away excess soap, leaving a thin, even coating for easy release of plaster casting. Following package directions for plaster of paris, mix 1 1/2 lbs. plaster to 12 oz. water to make a paste of medium moist consistency. Pour mixture into bottom of pan until plaster is about 3/4 inch thick. With your finger, add plaster to each candy mold cavity until half full. Tap pan and molds on table 5 or 6 times to release air bubbles.

For hanging wires on pan mold: Bend 5 inches florist wire, forming a 3 inch wide arch between two straight 1 inch wide sides. Bury straight sides half way into depth of plaster so that arch extends above surface. Smooth top surface of plaster with finger. Let air dry 3 hours or more until solid.

For hanging wires on candy molds: Bend a 1 1/2 inch piece of wire into a small arch between 2 horizontal sides, bury sides into mold, leaving arch exposed. Let air dry.

Fold a towel on table for casting to rest on. To release pan casting, bend pan out slightly on sides. Plaque should easily slide out.

To paint: Sand surface of plaque with sandpaper. To create a terra cotta look, mix White, Burnt Sienna and Yellow Ochre paints to achieve base color. Apply evenly over castings, using two coats if necessary. Lighten the remaining paint slightly by adding more white. Lightly dab this color with a paper towel onto the raised surfaces, avoiding the recessed areas. Continue lightly dabbing until you achieve a subtle 2-tone effect of weathered terra cotta.

Secure plaque to wreath at top and bottom, and candy molds by twisting more florist wire to back.

The Jolly Santa Pan also makes an unforgettable, edible candy plaque. Simply melt Wilton Candy Melts™ confectionery brand coating, pour into the pan and chill. You can also paint in colorful accents using decorators brushes before you fill the pan.

Credits

Creative Director............. Richard Tracy
Food Editor.....................Zella Junkin
Food Stylists
and Decorators..............Mary Helen Steindler
Kathy Kari
Sandy Folsom
Susan Matusiak
Steve Rocco
Mary Gavenda
Corky Kagay
Photography.....................Kathy Sanders
Photo Assistant................Cristin Nestor
Writers...........................Jeff Shankman
Mary Enochs
Marita Seiler
Production Coordinators.... Marie De Benedictis
Mary Stahulak
Production Art................ RNB Graphics

To order the Wilton Products used in this book, use the Order Form inside.
Those items not listed on the Order Form, such as tips and colors,
are available where Wilton products are sold. You can also write or call:

Wilton Enterprises
Caller Service 1604
2240 W. 75th St., Woodridge, IL 60517
1-708-963-7100

For photography purposes, some designs were decorated with royal icing.

Printed in U.S.A.

Wilton products used in this book are available through your Wilton dealer or the current Wilton Yearbook of Cake Decorating. You may also use this handy Order Form to purchase most products in this book.

How To Order

1 Print your name, address and phone number clearly. If you wish your order sent to another address, be sure to include that information in the area designated: "SHIP TO."

2 You may pay by check, money order or credit card (Only VISA MasterCard or Discover Card accepted.) SORRY, NO C.O.D. ORDERS. To charge an order to your VISA, MasterCard or Discover Card enter your charge card number in the boxes. Supply card expiration date and your signature. Orders will not be processed without this information.

Make checks payable to Wilton Enterprises.

Wilton Enterprises is not responsible for cash sent by mail.

Orders from outside U.S.A. must be paid in U.S. Funds only.

3 Fill in the number of items desired. If an item includes more than one piece, DO NOT list number of pieces. Example: 14 piece set is listed as 1 item under quantity.

4 Total your order.

5 Add appropiate amount to your order for shipping, handling and postage for inside U.S.A. (See chart inside Order Form to determine charges.) Wilton ships via United Parcel Service. Allow 10 working days for delivery. (HI and AK allow 17 working days.)

Outside the U.S.A. shipping, handling and postage totals $7.00. Allow 3 months for delivery (except Canada).

(see other side)

Order Form

(1) SOLD TO: (Please print plainly)

Name__________

Address__________

City__________ State_____ Zip_____

Daytime Phone No./Area Code_____-_____-_____

SHIP TO: (Fill in only if different from Sold To.)

Name__________

Address__________

City__________ State_____ Zip_____

Daytime Phone No./Area Code_____-_____-_____

(2) CREDIT CARD ORDERS: Use Visa, MasterCard, or Discover Card! Fill in the boxes: Credit Card Number

Expiration Month/Year_____ Signature__________

PANS

STOCK NO.	HOW MANY (3)	DESCRIPTION	PRICE OF ONE	TOTAL PRICE
2105-Z-2525		Angel Food Pan	$13.99 ea.	
2105-Z-2644		Even-Bake® Insulated Cookie Sheet 13x17"	$14.99 ea.	
2105-Z-2646		Even-Bake® Insulated Cookie Sheet 10x15"	$12.99 ea.	
2105-Z-2650		Even-Bake® Insulated Jelly Roll Pan	$17.99 ea.	
2105-Z-2669		Even-Bake® Insulated 8 " Round Pan	$12.99 ea.	
2105-Z-2664		Even-Bake® Insulated 7 x 11" Biscuit/Brownie Pan	$12.99 ea.	
2105-Z-5008		Fancy Ring Mold Pan	$ 9.99 ea.	
2105-Z-4854		Jelly Roll Pan (12 x 18")	$ 9.99 ea.	
2105-Z-1225		Jolly Santa Pan	$ 7.99 ea.	
2105-Z-4497		Mini Bear Pan	$ 9.99 ea.	
2105-Z-9791		Mini Loaf Pan	$ 9.99 ea.	
2105-Z-472		Mini Snowman Pan	$ 7.99 ea.	
2105-Z-1779		Mini Christmas Tree Pan	$ 7.99 ea.	
2105-Z-2125		Mini Muffin Pan	$ 7.49 ea.	
2105-Z-5338		Standard Muffin Pan	$ 7.49 ea.	
2105-Z-1820		Jumbo Muffin Pan	$12.99 ea.	
2105-Z-2130		Oval Pan Set (4 pc.)	$23.99 set	
2105-Z-603		Panda Pan	$16.99 set	
2105-Z-3903		Pizza Primo Pizza Pan (16")	$12.99 ea.	
2105-Z-4013		Ring Mold (10 1/2")	$ 7.99 ea.	
2105-Z-2193		Round Pan (8")	$ 5.49 ea.	
2105-Z-2207		Round Pan (10")	$ 6.49 ea.	
2105-Z-4432		Santa Bear Pan	$ 7.99 ea.	
2105-Z-158		Sheet Pan (11 x 15")	$10.99 ea.	
2105-Z-803		Snowman Pan	$ 7.99 ea.	
2105-Z-4437		Springform Pan (6")	$ 7.99 ea.	
2105-Z-5354		Springform Pan (9")	$10.99 ea.	
507-Z-2180		Square Pan (6")	$ 4.99 ea.	
2105-Z-8191		Square Pan (8")	$ 6.49 ea.	
2105-Z-8205		Square Pan (10")	$ 8.49 ea.	
2105-Z-2512		Star Pan	$ 9.99 ea.	
2105-Z-425		Treeliteful Pan	$ 7.99 ea.	
2105-Z-8252		Viennese Swirl Pan	$ 9.99 ea.	
2105-Z-565		Wonder Mold Pan Kit	$11.99 kit	

Order Form

(1) SOLD TO: (Please print plainly)

Name__________

Address__________

City__________ State_____ Zip_____

Daytime Phone No./Area Code_____-_____-_____

SHIP TO: (Fill in only if different from Sold To.)

Name__________

Address__________

City__________ State_____ Zip_____

Daytime Phone No./Area Code_____-_____-_____

(2) CREDIT CARD ORDERS: Use Visa, MasterCard, or Discover Card! Fill in the boxes: Credit Card Number

Expiration Month/Year_____ Signature__________

PANS

STOCK NO.	HOW MANY (3)	DESCRIPTION	PRICE OF ONE	TOTAL PRICE
2105-Z-2525		Angel Food Pan	$13.99 ea.	
2105-Z-2644		Even-Bake® Insulated Cookie Sheet 13x17"	$14.99 ea.	
2105-Z-2646		Even-Bake® Insulated Cookie Sheet 10x15"	$12.99 ea.	
2105-Z-2650		Even-Bake® Insulated Jelly Roll Pan	$17.99 ea.	
2105-Z-2669		Even-Bake® Insulated 8 " Round Pan	$12.99 ea.	
2105-Z-2664		Even-Bake® Insulated 7 x 11" Biscuit/Brownie Pan	$12.99 ea.	
2105-Z-5008		Fancy Ring Mold Pan	$ 9.99 ea.	
2105-Z-4854		Jelly Roll Pan (12 x 18")	$ 9.99 ea.	
2105-Z-1225		Jolly Santa Pan	$ 7.99 ea.	
2105-Z-4497		Mini Bear Pan	$ 9.99 ea.	
2105-Z-9791		Mini Loaf Pan	$ 9.99 ea.	
2105-Z-472		Mini Snowman Pan	$ 7.99 ea.	
2105-Z-1779		Mini Christmas Tree Pan	$ 7.99 ea.	
2105-Z-2125		Mini Muffin Pan	$ 7.49 ea.	
2105-Z-5338		Standard Muffin Pan	$ 7.49 ea.	
2105-Z-1820		Jumbo Muffin Pan	$12.99 ea.	
2105-Z-2130		Oval Pan Set (4 pc.)	$23.99 set	
2105-Z-603		Panda Pan	$16.99 set	
2105-Z-3903		Pizza Primo Pizza Pan (16")	$12.99 ea.	
2105-Z-4013		Ring Mold (10 1/2")	$ 7.99 ea.	
2105-Z-2193		Round Pan (8")	$ 5.49 ea.	
2105-Z-2207		Round Pan (10")	$ 6.49 ea.	
2105-Z-4432		Santa Bear Pan	$ 7.99 ea.	
2105-Z-158		Sheet Pan (11 x 15")	$10.99 ea.	
2105-Z-803		Snowman Pan	$ 7.99 ea.	
2105-Z-4437		Springform Pan (6")	$ 7.99 ea.	
2105-Z-5354		Springform Pan (9")	$10.99 ea.	
507-Z-2180		Square Pan (6")	$ 4.99 ea.	
2105-Z-8191		Square Pan (8")	$ 6.49 ea.	
2105-Z-8205		Square Pan (10")	$ 8.49 ea.	
2105-Z-2512		Star Pan	$ 9.99 ea.	
2105-Z-425		Treeliteful Pan	$ 7.99 ea.	
2105-Z-8252		Viennese Swirl Pan	$ 9.99 ea.	
2105-Z-565		Wonder Mold Pan Kit	$11.99 kit	

How To Order Continued

6 Add state and local taxes *where you live** to your total amount, including shipping and delivery charges. See Tax Chart below. Wilton Enterprises is required by law to collect state taxes on orders shipped to:

AZ 5%: CA 6.5%: CO 3.7%: FL 6%: GA 4%: IL 6.75%: IN 5%: KS 4.25%: KY 6%: LA 4%: MD 5%: MA 5%: MI 4%: MN 6%: MO 4.225%: NC 5%: NJ 7%: NY 7%: OH 6%: PA 6%: SD 6%: TN 7.75%: TX 8%: UT 6.25%: VA 4.5%: WA 7.5%.

*Tax rates are subject to change according to individual state legislation.

7 UPS Next Day and Second Day Service available upon request. Air Service outside U.S.A. add 100% of your cost.

8 When your order arrives...Should you be missing an item from your order (1) check to be sure you have not overlooked the merchandise (2) check over your receipted order form. If any item is temporarily out of stock we forward the balance of your order with out of stock notification and the reorder date. If payment is check or money order, you will recieve a credit memo for the amount of the missing item. The memo may be applied to your next order or returned to Customer Service for a cash refund. Charge Accounts will be charged only for merchandise shipped.

Wilton Return Policy: Inspect all merchandise upon arrival. If you're dissatisfied in any way with any item, notify Wilton Customer Service in writing with a copy of your invoice and all available information regarding your order before returning merchandise. A Customer Service Representative will contact you.

You have 60 days to return merchandise. Handle returns promptly, as they take approximately 30 days to process.

SAVE MAILING TIME! Phone in your charge order. 1-708-963-7100. Ask for mail order. Remember! Only charge orders (VISA, MasterCard or Discover Card) will be accepted by phone.

Prices in this book supersede all previous Wilton publications. Wilton reserves the right to change prices without notice.

For inquiries on your previous order, send all available information and a copy of your invoice to:

Wilton Enterprises
2240 West 75th Street
Woodridge, IL 60517
1-708-963-7100
A Wilton Industries Company

CANDY

STOCK NO.	HOW MANY (3)	DESCRIPTION	PRICE OF ONE	TOTAL PRICE
1911-Z-498		Candy Melts-White (14 oz. bag)	$2.50 ea.	
2114-Z-94136		Christmas I Molds	$1.99 ea.	
2114-Z-94152		Christmas II Molds	$1.99 ea.	
2114-Z-1224		Christmas Classics Set I	$3.99 set	
2114-Z-1225		Christmas Classics Set II	$3.99 set	
2114-Z-91099		Christmas Trees	$1.99 ea.	
COOKIES				
2304-Z-802		Christmas Cookie Cutters (10pc.)	$3.99 set	
2304-Z-801		Christmas Favorites Cookie Cutters (4 pc.)	$2.99 set	
2303-Z-97		Giant Gingerbread Boy Cutter	$1.50 ea.	
2303-Z-96		Giant Tree Cutter	$1.50 ea.	
2304-Z-121		Gingerbread Family Cutters (4 pc.)	$2.99 set	
2304-Z-1531		Nesting Christmas Tree Set(4 pc.)	$2.99 set	
2304-Z-113		Nesting Round Cutter Set (6 pc.)	$2.99 set	
2304-Z-111		Nesting Star Cutter Set (6 pc.)	$2.99 set	
2304-Z-1520		Nesting Bear Cutter Set (4 pc.)	$2.99 set	
2303-Z-139		Perimeter Locomotive Engine Cutter	.69 ea.	
2303-Z-127		Perimeter Rocking Horse Cutter	.69 ea.	
2303-Z-114		Perimeter Roller Skate Cutter	.69 ea.	
2303-Z-129		Perimeter Sailboat Cutter	.69 ea.	
2303-Z-133		Perimeter Teddy Bear Cutter	.69 ea.	
2104-Z-4000		Spritz Cookie Press	$10.99 set	
TOPPERS				
2113-Z-2015		Appaloosa Rocking Horse Set (4)	$3.49 set	
2113-Z-9004		Train Cake Top Set (12)	$2.49 set	
2811-Z-9131		Darling Dolls Candles Set (4)	$2.99 set	
2811-Z-214		Party Teddy Bear Candle Set (4)	$2.99 set	
2113-Z-2333		Derby Clowns Set (6)	$2.49 set	
1008-Z-726		Message Cake Picks (2)	$1.39 set	
OTHER				
409-Z-800		Cake Dividing Set	$8.99 set	
604-Z-2237		Clear Vanilla Extract (2 oz.)	$1.79 ea.	
701-Z-47		Color Flow Mix (4 oz. can)	$7.49 ea.	
2104-Z-846		Decorator Brush Set (3)	$1.49 set	
409-Z-990		Decorating Comb	.99 ea.	
399-Z-801		Dowel Rods (pack of 4, plastic)	$2.29 ea.	
703-Z-1204		Edible Glitter (1/4 oz. jar)	$2.29 ea.	
417-Z-9500		Flower Former Set	$5.99 set	
2104-Z-1525		Gingerbread House Kit	$7.49 kit	
707-Z-109		Glucose (24 oz. jar)	$4.29 ea.	
708-Z-14		Glycerine (2 oz.)	$1.99 ea.	
2104-Z-10		Make Any Message Letter Press Set	$7.99 set	
702-Z-6007		Meringue Powder (4 oz.)	$4.49 ea.	
702-Z-6015		Meringue Powder (8 oz.)	$6.99 ea.	
417-Z-1150		Tree Former Set	$1.99 set	

MONEY BACK GUARANTEE
If you are not completely satisfied with your Wilton purchase, return the item for an exchange or refund.

4	TOTAL MERCHANDISE		
5	ADD SHIPPING, HANDLING & POSTAGE CHARGE. NOTE! Find the amount you pay on chart below.		
6	STATE AND LOCAL TAXES-SEE TAX NOTE		
7	SPECIAL SHIPPING SERVICES		
	SUBTOTAL		
8	COUPONS AND/OR CREDIT MEMO DEDUCTIONS		
	TOTAL AMOUNT ENCLOSED		

FOR OFFICE USE ONLY. Please do not write in spaces below.

Date	Cash	Debit M.	Credit M.	Hndlng Charge
Air Mail	Foreign	Pal/Sam	Coupon	Gift Ct.

Shipping and Handling Charges (See No. 5)
Orders up to $29.99......add $3.50
Orders from $30-49.99 add $4.00
Orders from $50-74.99 add $5.00
Orders $75 and more.... add $6.00

CANDY

STOCK NO.	HOW MANY (3)	DESCRIPTION	PRICE OF ONE	TOTAL PRICE
1911-Z-498		Candy Melts-White (14 oz. bag)	$2.50 ea.	
2114-Z-94136		Christmas I Molds	$1.99 ea.	
2114-Z-94152		Christmas II Molds	$1.99 ea.	
2114-Z-1224		Christmas Classics Set I	$3.99 set	
2114-Z-1225		Christmas Classics Set II	$3.99 set	
2114-Z-91099		Christmas Trees	$1.99 ea.	
COOKIES				
2304-Z-802		Christmas Cookie Cutters (10pc.)	$3.99 set	
2304-Z-801		Christmas Favorites Cookie Cutters (4 pc.)	$2.99 set	
2303-Z-97		Giant Gingerbread Boy Cutter	$1.50 ea.	
2303-Z-96		Giant Tree Cutter	$1.50 ea.	
2304-Z-121		Gingerbread Family Cutters (4 pc.)	$2.99 set	
2304-Z-1531		Nesting Christmas Tree Set(4 pc.)	$2.99 set	
2304-Z-113		Nesting Round Cutter Set (6 pc.)	$2.99 set	
2304-Z-111		Nesting Star Cutter Set (6 pc.)	$2.99 set	
2304-Z-1520		Nesting Bear Cutter Set (4 pc.)	$2.99 set	
2303-Z-139		Perimeter Locomotive Engine Cutter	.69 ea.	
2303-Z-127		Perimeter Rocking Horse Cutter	.69 ea.	
2303-Z-114		Perimeter Roller Skate Cutter	.69 ea.	
2303-Z-129		Perimeter Sailboat Cutter	.69 ea.	
2303-Z-133		Perimeter Teddy Bear Cutter	.69 ea.	
2104-Z-4000		Spritz Cookie Press	$10.99 set	
TOPPERS				
2113-Z-2015		Appaloosa Rocking Horse Set (4)	$3.49 set	
2113-Z-9004		Train Cake Top Set (12)	$2.49 set	
2811-Z-9131		Darling Dolls Candles Set (4)	$2.99 set	
2811-Z-214		Party Teddy Bear Candle Set (4)	$2.99 set	
2113-Z-2333		Derby Clowns Set (6)	$2.49 set	
1008-Z-726		Message Cake Picks (2)	$1.39 set	
OTHER				
409-Z-800		Cake Dividing Set	$8.99 set	
604-Z-2237		Clear Vanilla Extract (2 oz.)	$1.79 ea.	
701-Z-47		Color Flow Mix (4 oz. can)	$7.49 ea.	
2104-Z-846		Decorator Brush Set (3)	$1.49 set	
409-Z-990		Decorating Comb	.99 ea.	
399-Z-801		Dowel Rods (pack of 4, plastic)	$2.29 ea.	
703-Z-1204		Edible Glitter (1/4 oz. jar)	$2.29 ea.	
417-Z-9500		Flower Former Set	$5.99 set	
2104-Z-1525		Gingerbread House Kit	$7.49 kit	
707-Z-109		Glucose (24 oz. jar)	$4.29 ea.	
708-Z-14		Glycerine (2 oz.)	$1.99 ea.	
2104-Z-10		Make Any Message Letter Press Set	$7.99 set	
702-Z-6007		Meringue Powder (4 oz.)	$4.49 ea.	
702-Z-6015		Meringue Powder (8 oz.)	$6.99 ea.	
417-Z-1150		Tree Former Set	$1.99 set	

MONEY BACK GUARANTEE
If you are not completely satisfied with your Wilton purchase, return the item for an exchange or refund.

4	TOTAL MERCHANDISE		
5	ADD SHIPPING, HANDLING & POSTAGE CHARGE. NOTE! Find the amount you pay on chart below.		
6	STATE AND LOCAL TAXES-SEE TAX NOTE		
7	SPECIAL SHIPPING SERVICES		
	SUBTOTAL		
8	COUPONS AND/OR CREDIT MEMO DEDUCTIONS		
	TOTAL AMOUNT ENCLOSED		

FOR OFFICE USE ONLY. Please do not write in spaces below.

Date	Cash	Debit M.	Credit M.	Hndlng Charge
Air Mail	Foreign	Pal/Sam	Coupon	Gift Ct.

Shipping and Handling Charges (See No. 5)
Orders up to $29.99......add $3.50
Orders from $30-49.99 add $4.00
Orders from $50-74.99 add $5.00
Orders $75 and more.... add $6.00